Praise for

'Everyone would benefit from reading Judkins, if only because he is so entertaining . . . His chapters are packed with counterintuitive insights and hard truths, which are seldom so clearly and vividly laid out' – *Psychology Today*

'Whatever your creative hangup, Rod Judkins has steps you can take now, and a wealth of examples to support his advice. An admirably straightforward, no-nonsense guide to getting over yourself and getting to work' – Mason Currey, author of *Daily Rituals: How Artists Work*

'This book is packed with great stories and ideas to power up your work journey with creativity and success by doing things differently' – Susie Pearl, author of *The Art of Creativity* and *Instructions for Happiness and Success*

'As thrilling as it is useful, Rod Judkin's latest manifesto on how to lead the creative life is . . . full of left-field thinking and case studies that illustrate the path of success . . . I loved it' – Phil Beadle, educator and author of *How to Teach*

Make Brilliant Work

Rod Judkins is a lecturer at Central Saint Martins in London, one of the world's pre-eminent art schools whose alumni range from Lucian Freud and Antony Gormley to Stella McCartney and Alexander McQueen. He has lectured on the subject of creativity at universities and to businesses around the world. Trained at the Royal College of Art, he has exhibited at galleries including Tate Britain, the National Portrait Gallery and the Royal Academy of Arts. As well as writing *Make Brilliant Work*, Rod has published three other books – including *The Art of Creative Thinking*, which is an international bestseller – and has been published in fifteen languages.

Also By Rod Judkins

Make Brilliant Work

Lessons on Creativity, Innovation, and Success

Rod Judkins

PAN BOOKS

First published 2021 by Macmillan

This paperback edition first published 2022 by Pan Books
an imprint of Pan Macmillan
The Smithson, 6 Briset Street, London EC1M 5NR
EU *representative*: Macmillan Publishers Ireland Ltd,
1st Floor, The Liffey Trust Centre,
117–126 Sheriff Street Upper,
Dublin 1, D01 YC43

ISBN 978-1-5290-6015-7

1 3 5 7 9 8 6 4 2

A CIP catalogue record for this book is available from the British Library.

Illustrations © Rod Judkins

Typeset by Palimpsest Book Production Ltd, Falkirk, Stirlingshire
Printed and bound by CPI Group (UK) Ltd, Croydon, CR0 4YY

Visit **www.panmacmillan.com** to read more about all our books
and to buy them. You will also find features, author interviews and
news of any author events, and you can sign up for e-newsletters
so that you're always first to hear about our new releases.

For Zelda, Scarlet and Louis

Contents

How do we rate work?

'It's bad,'

'It's good,'

Or 'It's brilliant.'

What response does your work usually get? Be honest.

This book will show you how to ensure your work is brilliant.

Introduction

You don't have to be brilliant to produce brilliant work. Many of the characters you will meet in this book failed at school, lacked natural talent, were not especially gifted or were repeatedly sacked. But their methods produced brilliant work – and they will work for you, too.

For the last twenty years, I have taught the techniques in this book to students at Central Saint Martins in London, one of the world's leading art and design universities, helping them tap into a reservoir of unused potential. And when I give talks and workshops at some of the world's most successful companies, such as Apple, Samsung and Porsche, I draw on these stories to inspire creativity. Now I want to share them with you.

Whether you are a business or an individual, you might find it hard to produce something significant and important. The real-life heroes in this book will show you how to make the transformation from ordinary to extraordinary. The longer you carry on working in the same way, the deeper into the rut of mediocrity you might get. Don't expect help – it's down to you. So if your work is good but not brilliant, or if you feel like you're dying inside as you sit through another meeting or a dreary PowerPoint presentation, now is the time to act.

Adopt a gladiator mindset

Anyone wanting to produce brilliant work needs to adopt a gladiator mindset. A gladiator in ancient Rome needed intelligence, skill and a strong will – qualities that underpin any significant project. You have to shield your work against attacks while simultaneously fighting back.

In the 1990s, a painful professional blow struck the architect Zaha Hadid. Her design for the Cardiff Bay Opera House had won the competition. It was her big breakthrough moment – architects and design experts agreed it would be the most original and compelling building in Britain, looking like jewels around the neck of an opera singer. Yet the narrow-minded politicians and bureaucrats in control of the funding cancelled the project.

Hadid was devastated, yet she fought back with even more proposals for projects across the globe. A pattern emerged. Architects and designers considered her designs the best, and she won the commissions. But committees in charge of decision-making lost their nerve and backed down.

Still, she didn't become discouraged, despite the many years when her ideas were considered impossible to transform into bricks and mortar. Only when a Hadid design was eventually built, the Vitra Fire Station in Weil am Rhein, Germany, did the floodgates open. Suddenly everyone wanted her to design a landmark building.

I had the privilege of meeting Hadid at Central Saint Martins when she came in to talk to my students. She was a lively and commanding presence. Before her talk, she had a strong coffee and a bag of potato crisps, and before eating a crisp she held it up and rotated it slowly to scrutinize its curved geometry from different angles.

I had set my art students an architecture project. Rather than design a building on paper, I asked them to dive straight in and make models with whatever materials they found in the studio; not only traditional mediums like cardboard and clay, but things like coffee cups or bubble wrap. I limited them to twenty minutes to make the model. Their rough, raw models fascinated Hadid, and she loved the idea of working quickly and instinctively, an attribute she felt in danger of losing given her role as CEO of a multimillion-dollar company. Despite her fame and success, her interest in the work was intense. She also knew that I was a painter, and bombarded me with questions about glazes, washes and the techniques of various artists. She saw an opportunity to learn, absorbing anything that could make her work stronger and more brilliant.

Hadid had the steely determination of a fighter. She wasn't born with this ability – she developed it. As an Iranian woman in the competitive and male-dominated world of architecture, she

Weapons of mass creation

5

had to overcome obstacle after obstacle. She intentionally developed her gladiator mindset so that her personality shone through in her work – a determination to be true to herself and her vision, no matter what. Look around you: most objects are symmetrical. Hadid used asymmetry to make her designs dramatic and eye-catching. Although committees had been afraid of the asymmetry in her work, Hadid stuck to her guns. She didn't strive for balance but aimed for unbalanced.

Dare to create instability. Unbalance your audience by keeping them on edge. Punctuate long, quiet periods in a song with short, loud sections, or leave a large blank area of a painting next to a finely wrought area. Every element in your work – its colour, size or texture – has a weight. Symmetry divides these elements equally either side of a centreline, making it predictable and humdrum. An asymmetrical design has different loads. It will make your work more dynamic and surprising. In Hadid's brilliant design for a 128-metre yacht, in association with the German shipbuilder Blohm+Voss, each side was different, but the weight was distributed equally. Instead of the usual horizontal lines, Hadid connected the decks with diagonals, to create a dynamic object that suited its dynamic environment.

The committee of Welsh politicians and bureaucrats played it safe and refused to fund the Cardiff Bay Opera House. When their Chinese counterparts later commissioned the Guangzhou Opera House from Hadid, they helped transform their city into a cultural capital that declares Guangzhou to be a modern, forward-looking city, unafraid of new ideas. In 2004 Hadid became the first woman to win the prestigious Pritzker Architecture Prize since it was first awarded in 1979, and more prizes followed. When she won the Royal Gold

Medal for Architecture in 2016, she said, 'As a woman in architecture, you're always an outsider. It's OK, I like being on the edge.' Once, Hadid had a reputation for designing unbuildable buildings; now, she has earned a reputation for building the unbuildable.

1 It's not enough to produce work, sit back and hope it will be appreciated. You have to build a gladiator mindset so that you can fight for it. Hadid's gladiator attitude is essential for anyone in any field – she didn't complain about her situation, she picked up her sword and fought and proved how good she was through her work.

2 We must know when to fight for our work. We all suffer blows and injuries to our ego in the fight for what we believe in. No one else is going to risk everything for your work. It's down to you to pick up the sword. 'People don't understand the kind of fight it takes to record what you want to record the way you want to record it,' said Billie Holiday.

Think like a guerrilla – lessons in counterinsurgency

Don't assume brilliant work will get attention because it's brilliant. Great achievements can go unnoticed in a busy, chaotic world. If you produce something you're proud of, make sure the spotlight shines on it. Sometimes we're concentrating so hard on doing brilliant work that we forget to look up and make sure it's getting recognition.

In 1939, the artist Salvador Dalí was arrested in New York and charged with malicious mischief. He smashed a huge plate-glass window of the department store Bonwit Teller. The store had hired Dalí to produce some art for their windows. He created surreal scenes with naked mannequins, a bathtub with buffalo legs, and other strange combinations. They were so outrageous that when he left to set up an exhibition in a gallery, the store changed his work.

When Dalí returned to Bonwit Teller and saw the alterations, he was furious. He jumped into the display and tried to rearrange it, crashing the bathtub through the window. No one was injured, but the police arrested Dalí. The judge handed him a suspended sentence because he believed that 'every artist has the right to defend their work.'

An angry mob gathered outside Dalí's New York gallery exhibition before it opened, frustrated because they wanted to get inside and buy his work. The connection between negative publicity and positive sales impressed Dalí.

When Dalí was promoting an exhibition in London, he delivered a talk dressed in a deep-sea diving costume. There was a point to the stunt: the theme of his speech was diving deep into the unconscious. The crowd was thrilled as he staggered about, arms flailing. To their delight, he eventually collapsed. It took a while before everyone realized he was suffocating from lack of oxygen, because he didn't understand how diving suits worked. The other artists struggled to get the helmet off. On the opening day of the exhibition, the crowds were so huge outside that they stopped the traffic in Piccadilly. More publicity!

In person Dalí was shy, quiet, and disliked self-promotion. But his exhibitions took him months to put together, so he'd do anything to make sure they received attention. He accepted publicity as a necessary evil. There's nothing more frustrating than producing brilliant work, only for no one to notice.

When Dalí's friend and barber threw a party to celebrate the opening of his new barbershop, his press releases and ads didn't make an impact, so he asked Dalí to attend, knowing he'd attract the press. Dalí posed with the barber for a crowd of photographers. 'How much publicity do you want?' asked Dalí. 'As much as I can get,' replied the barber. Dalí thought for a moment. Then he picked up a hammer and walked towards the shop's front window.

Dalí abandoned traditional publicity techniques and instead created guerrilla tactics, paving the way for artists like Warhol, Jeff Koons and Damien Hirst to become media icons. Dalí spent 99 per cent of his time on his artworks and 1 per cent on publicity. But he made sure that 1 per cent had a significant impact. People from all walks of life soon realized they could use the same tactics.

It's an unpleasant truth that creating great work isn't enough. I've seen many of my most talented students go unnoticed because they didn't promote their work. It's frustrating for me because I want them to succeed and I know they could – if only they'd understand that getting attention is part of their job.

1   Don't let your work go unnoticed. It's your responsibility to ensure your work connects with the right audience. Please don't assume a brilliant idea will be adopted when shown to your organization or audience. You must frame your concept so it's understood, accepted and put into action. Dalí had an introverted personality, but he appreciated the necessity of overcoming his shyness and promoting his work. He would do whatever it took to get maximum exposure. Would you? Be eye-catching, but focus on communicating your message, and not attracting attention for its own sake.

2   Get support. Find an agent or manager to help you. Gala was Dalí's life partner and manager. She helped him to promote himself and to be more and more outrageous. Early in his career, Gala organized a 'Zodiac' club. There were twelve members, and each month one agreed to buy a Dalí painting for 2,500 francs (a lot of money at the time), which ensured him a stable income.

3   Explain yourself. Make your ideas public – write a blog or post on social media. Dalí wrote and published three diaries, one titled *Diary of a Genius* (1963), in which he wrote revealing facts and promoted his work and philosophy.

4   Make sure your work has substance. Attention is not a goal in itself; the purpose is to guide people to your work. Remember that you are trying to achieve something of worth.

Sometimes when I'm trying to promote a book (like this one), I find myself absorbed in social media and lose sight of the real purpose, which is to explain how these ideas are useful. Dalí's stunts were shocking, but focused on revealing his surrealist ideas. Make sure your self-promotion fits with your message.

5 Make your promotion memorable and relevant. Dalí's deep-sea diver stunt is still written about in art history books because it was connected to his work.

6 Don't set out to upset or annoy. You might want to shock, but ultimately you want people to enjoy and share your work with friends. Dalí was witty and charming, not annoying. Don't act out of character just for attention – Dalí was true to himself.

Enjoy the lows as much as the highs

It's essential to develop a strategy for dealing with your life's highs and lows. Research shows our mind has evolved to cope with difficulties by avoiding them. We avoid the pain caused by low points, but it stops us from taking action that would enable us to fulfil our potential.

In the future, you'll feel the pain of missed opportunities. The exhibitions, tech start-ups, films, businesses, social media platforms, and albums you didn't attempt will haunt you. It's not about being a great success; it's about knowing you tried and did your best.

Launching any important creative project takes courage. Many things can go wrong, and some usually do. If you care deeply, your emotions will soar up and down. You cannot achieve something worthwhile without experiencing emotional highs and lows. Whether you are creating a business start-up, an art installation, a climate change project, a science project, writing a novel or recording an album, you'll have to deal with setbacks if you care about a project.

In the 1970s, a film director had problems with a temperamental star who was always late, wouldn't follow the most straightforward directions, and had frequent breakdowns. An entire team was devoted to getting the star on set, pampering them and tending to their every need. The star ate up the film's budget. Each day, the director scoured the rushes, but the lead actor's volatile antics ruined most scenes. The actors, film crew and producers regretted committing to a movie dominated by a mechanical shark.

The film's director, Steven Spielberg, wanted Hollywood to take him seriously and was desperate for *Jaws* to make an impact. For any creative person, it's important to control your emotions and focus on what you need to do. And to achieve that, it's essential to figure out a strategy to deal with the lows and the highs.

High: Universal Studios had asked Spielberg to direct *Jaws*. It was a big-budget movie and an opportunity to show he could handle the big time.

Low: Spielberg felt there were problems with the script. He believed an audience only became genuinely involved in a film if there were people to root for, but the audience rooted for the shark in this film. Many rewrites were done by many different writers, and they had to start shooting without a finished script.

Low: Richard Dreyfuss, although a little-known actor at the time, turned down his role three times. He didn't like the script or his character because he had to dispense an endless stream of shark facts.

High: Dreyfuss eventually accepted the role. His previous film had been a flop, so, worried he'd never get another role, he took the part with huge reservations. He said later, 'We started the film without a script, without a cast, and without a shark.'

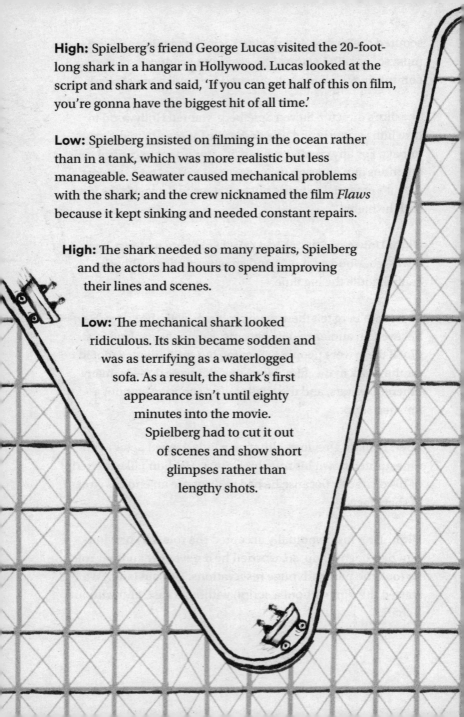

High: Spielberg's friend George Lucas visited the 20-foot-long shark in a hangar in Hollywood. Lucas looked at the script and shark and said, 'If you can get half of this on film, you're gonna have the biggest hit of all time.'

Low: Spielberg insisted on filming in the ocean rather than in a tank, which was more realistic but less manageable. Seawater caused mechanical problems with the shark; and the crew nicknamed the film *Flaws* because it kept sinking and needed constant repairs.

High: The shark needed so many repairs, Spielberg and the actors had hours to spend improving their lines and scenes.

Low: The mechanical shark looked ridiculous. Its skin became sodden and was as terrifying as a waterlogged sofa. As a result, the shark's first appearance isn't until eighty minutes into the movie. Spielberg had to cut it out of scenes and show short glimpses rather than lengthy shots.

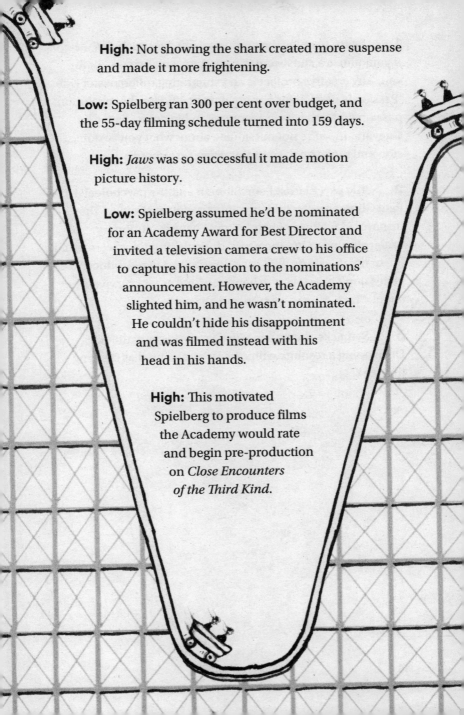

High: Not showing the shark created more suspense and made it more frightening.

Low: Spielberg ran 300 per cent over budget, and the 55-day filming schedule turned into 159 days.

High: *Jaws* was so successful it made motion picture history.

Low: Spielberg assumed he'd be nominated for an Academy Award for Best Director and invited a television camera crew to his office to capture his reaction to the nominations' announcement. However, the Academy slighted him, and he wasn't nominated. He couldn't hide his disappointment and was filmed instead with his head in his hands.

High: This motivated Spielberg to produce films the Academy would rate and begin pre-production on *Close Encounters of the Third Kind*.

1   Learn to enjoy the emotional lows as much as the highs. If your aim is a consistent, happy state, creativity is not for you. Any creative project is an exhilarating rollercoaster ride. 'Passion is needed for any great work, and for the revolution, passion and audacity are required in big doses,' said Che Guevara. If you're not passionate about what you're doing, stop and move on to something you care about.

2   The psychiatrist Leon Sloman and the psychologist Paul Gilbert researched 'involuntary defeat strategy'. They discovered feelings of helplessness have evolutionary underpinnings. Our ancestors' difficult situations were usually life or death – those who gave up survived to reproduce. Your genes don't care if you're happy so long as you survive. They shout, 'Take the easy option and give up.'

3   Setbacks strengthen you if you overcome them. Developing a resolute willpower is as essential as creating the work.

Transform ordinary
into extraordinary

It's easy to fall into the trap of fire-fighting – dealing with small, urgent problems and doing just enough to get by. That's why most of our work is ordinary. We get bogged down in satisfying short-term needs and lose the ambition to produce extraordinary work.

If your work is ordinary, there's a solution – add 'extra' to ordinary. Maybe you feel you're an ordinary person doing an ordinary job in an ordinary way. Decide to do something 'extra', and you're on your way to becoming 'extra' ordinary. 'Extra' is from the Latin, meaning 'beyond, better than the ordinary'. It's not enough to fulfil the brief. Be generous. Go above and beyond what's expected of you.

A firm of Italian architects responded to a competition to design a bridge. They created a power station – with a bridge attached. Architects Francesco Colarossi, Giovanna Saracino and Luisa Saracino designed the 'Solar Wind' bridge, which had twenty-six wind turbines added to the structure and solar cells embedded in the roadway and could generate enough renewable energy to power thousands of homes. They went the extra mile and solved more than the problem of crossing from one side to the other. Don't see your goal as fulfilling the client's brief; see your goal as producing something extraordinary.

Artist Tom Phillips started his project *A Humument* in 1966. The task he set himself was to find a second-hand book and paint or collage onto every page to create an entirely new version. The book he used was an obscure Victorian oddity, and he added a page to it every week for years. Phillips' first version was printed in 1973, and he has continuously developed it into an extraordinary, fascinating work. It is his masterpiece and what he is most known for. It was an epic undertaking, but that was the point: to set himself a huge challenge. By constantly adding a little bit to it every week, over the weeks and years it has grown into an awesome work of breathtaking scale.

An exponent of the 'extra' mindset is technology entrepreneur Elon Musk, who has said, 'I think it's possible for ordinary people to choose to be extraordinary.' Musk's achievements are exceptional because he believed he could make himself do extraordinary things. When designing the Tesla electric car, he dreamed up extras, and used computer technology to ensure a Tesla could be years old and still have all the latest features. The Tesla's first innovation was to be self-driving, and Musk regularly added extra features. These include enabling the Tesla to talk to pedestrians; 'Sentry Mode', which takes videos of anyone who goes near the vehicle; 'Enhanced Summon', which can park it in tight spaces; and 'Stop Light Warning', which alerts you if it looks like you might accidentally shoot through a red light. 'Chill Mode' is for a smooth, gentle ride.

I've worked with CEOs of major organizations in my work for The Future Group (a bespoke executive education programme designed for future business leaders wanting to develop their leadership skills), as well as some of the world's most significant and innovative companies such as Apple and Samsung. In everyday life, the leaders are surprisingly ordinary, but at work, they desperately want to produce something extraordinary. When I work with them, I try to instil a simple principle: relentlessly think of features you can add to your product or service. I once worked as a creative consultant for a business that produced and sold cars. We added a financing arm to help customers finance their purchases, which grew to the point where it was more lucrative than car sales. As a result, the company dropped the car sales because the enterprise was so complicated and required so much space. Instead, they focused on the finance – but kept adding extra attributes.

The 'extra' mindset was a huge attribute of the sculptor Eduardo Paolozzi. He was a tutor at the Royal College of Art when I was a student there, and he used to be very generous to collectors. If they bought one of his sculptures, he'd often give them some drawings and maquettes that had been used in the development of the work. They'd hang them in their homes to show the history of the sculpture. It was instinctive generosity by Paolozzi, but I noticed it was also a good marketing ploy – though he would never have thought of it like that. 'Business strategy' would have been an anathema to him – but it *was* good business. The collectors were drawn to buy more sculptures because they got so many extras.

Adopting the 'extra' mindset can transform your life and work. In 1891, a young man started a business selling scouring soap. He offered customers an extra as an enticement to buy his soap – a can of free baking powder. But the baking powder was more popular than his soap, so he decided to sell only baking powder, instead giving his customers free chewing gum with each can. Once again, the free item proved more popular than the one being sold, and William Wrigley decided to sell only chewing gum from then on. The lesson being, if your project is ordinary, add extras. The point is transformation – to make the sublime out of something commonplace.

1   Train yourself to reject the ordinary and accept only the extraordinary. Don't be afraid of producing something strange, different, or exceptional – be scared of creating something ordinary. Think unusual thoughts, and it will lead to extraordinary creations. Make the most of your abilities and talents by discarding your everyday ideas and keep thinking until the extraordinary arrives. The goal is not to amass an Elon Musk-scale fortune, but to get the most out of your talents.

2   Do your ideas frighten you? If not, they're too predictable. Reasonable people have achievable dreams because they fear failure, looking foolish and hard work. Successful people have goals that scare them. People around you will find a way to justify taking the regular route; you'll have to force yourself to keep going beyond what you promised.

3   What can you add to your project? Add to your skills and knowledge every day, and you'll be able to add extras to your work. What can you learn that will make a new field accessible to you? Thinking extraordinary thoughts can become an everyday experience. If it's not remarkable, it's not worth doing.

Become an addict

Nature has installed an internal safety valve in us. We work within our limits, stop when we feel tired, take a coffee break when we can, and find ways to unwind. With this attitude, we only achieve the achievable.

The obsessive override their internal safety valve. Scratch the surface of a successful person, and you'll find compulsion. It doesn't matter if you have a low level of talent because a ridiculous, insane obsessiveness for your work will elevate you to the top level in your profession. You can produce brilliant work without ability as long as you apply obsession to the project. But no matter how talented you are, you can't create excellent work without obsession.

'Obsessed' has become a derogatory word. 'Obsessed' is how the idle label the devoted – the obsessive throw themselves entirely into work with positivity and fascination. The compulsive work long after others have stopped. Work on what you're most interested in, or you're working on the wrong thing.

Imagine a fashion designer who tirelessly worked night and day, produced several detailed drawings of every garment, wasn't content with the standard catwalk show, and instead built obsessively elaborate environments for the models to walk through. Instead of the usual runway, they would build an underwater world or a French country house, with real grass, ponds and trees. Someone that obsessive would dominate the fashion world – like Karl Lagerfeld.

When the young Lagerfeld was appointed designer at Fendi, he transformed it from a small luxury brand into a global phenomenon. He became head designer to the 'near-dead' brand Chanel when it had been in decline for years. Lagerfeld reinvigorated Chanel, made it relevant again, and boosted revenues to US$4 billion per year. 'He's a compulsive and obsessive artist, and it's contagious,' said actress Kristen Stewart. People admire the dedicated and driven. We must search for that driving need within us, and be driven not by shallow interests – to impress others, to earn money – but by a deep, worthy need to make the world a better, more beautiful place.

Lagerfeld's fashion shows reflected contemporary and political topics, such as freedom or the environment. At the age of seventy-nine, he launched eight collections at Chanel and five at Fendi and two for his personal brand – fifteen shows. He also published a book of his photography, one of several he produced during his career. All this within just one year. He was livelier and more engaged than most twenty-year-olds. Although he died aged eighty-five, he had signed a contract with one fashion brand that committed him until he was 105.

Lagerfeld often became obsessed with a particular era, concept or technology and mined it for ideas. Indeed, he became so obsessed with iPods that he amassed over 100. Lagerfeld's library, which contained over 300,000 books, was a complex construction of rolling ladders and spiral staircases. Instead of shelving books horizontally, he stacked them vertically because it was easier to read the titles. His library and photography were a resource he fed off; he realized that it's not enough to like something, you have to obsessively consume it. If you build up your work, your work builds you. The good things you make, make you good.

We have a choice: the quiet life of underachievement, or the hard life of pushing ourselves until we fulfil our potential. Bill Gates slept on the floor of his office because going home used up too much time. While you're unwinding, the obsessive are winding up because they work beyond their limits. Michelangelo worked eighteen hours a day painting *The Last Judgement* on the ceiling of the Sistine Chapel. He slept in his clothes, and when he finally took his boots off, the skin on his feet came off too. To reach an elevated level requires elevated commitment. We must try every option possible and maintain our enthusiasm. The great designer Philippe Starck explained, 'from the 15th of June to the 15th of September, I live completely secluded, locked in one of my houses, working from 8 in the morning to 8 at night, or making my own biorhythm: work three hours, sleep 45 minutes, work three hours, sleep 45 minutes, for 24 hours, without eating. It's a little sick.' Great creative successes are the result of persisting when others have given in to distractions and discouragement.

A compulsion pushes you to find your strengths and then share them. Decisions are more straightforward if you direct everything towards achieving your goals. You'll take responsibility for making every aspect of your work brilliant. Most artists have the same compulsive behaviours as drug addicts or alcoholics. The difference is that the artist makes sure they are addicted to something positive. Both are dealing with their inner demons and struggling with themselves, but the addict is avoiding their true calling by pouring all their effort into something worthless. One is easy; the other is hard. Being melodramatic is easy. Writing a play is hard. An addict or an art addict? The artist faces up to their compulsive behaviour and their fears; the addict panders to them.

1 Only work on the subject that interests you the most. If you're not obsessive about what you're doing, you're wasting your time on something temporary. Obsession is different from being a workaholic. A workaholic mindlessly slaves away. A passion isn't about becoming a self-made millionaire but finding what you care about deeply and putting your heart into it. Working to your highest level gives you enormous belief in yourself and your work. Dedication to your own highest standards will make your job more rewarding – work all day and night, speak out when something isn't good enough, and insist every detail is excellent.

2 Don't waste time on anything unimportant. Without an obsession, you're not making the most of your time. Your work must be what you most enjoy doing. People who work hard go far. The obsessive go further than far. When I was writing this book, I wrote wherever and whenever possible. I often woke up in the middle of the night, wondered why, and then realized I'd had an idea in my sleep and typed up the idea. It's the only way – you can't drift in and out of a project, you must keep it at the forefront of your mind.

3 Finish a project. Don't start a project unless you're obsessed with it. Finish the project once you've started; don't let it drift on unresolved. Throw yourself into finishing it as if your life depended on it. The ability to see something through to the end is crucial – if you don't complete a project, it can haunt you. For your work to stand out, you'll have to work much harder than everyone else.

4 Develop compulsive creative disorder. People won't care about your work until they see how much *you* care about your work. Resist the pressure to use cheap materials, cut corners, or do things you know you shouldn't – even if they could bring short-term profit. Be obsessed with the highest quality. Think of people you admire in politics, sport, the arts, business or science. They were high achievers, not because they were obsessed with making money, success or fame, but because they cared about achieving something worthwhile.

Turn insults into results

Rejection stings – we've all experienced the pain. Rebuttal makes some people give up, but somehow the successful find a way to bounce back stronger. How you react is essential, and rejection can be your best teacher if you use strong emotions to your benefit. The right attitude can transform the wrong response into the right result.

In 1977, unknown guitarist and producer Nile Rodgers was invited to the 'hippest place on the planet', the legendary and ultra-exclusive Studio 54 in New York. A bouncer hadn't received the updated guest list and slammed the door in his face, telling him to 'f**k off'. Most people would shuffle away and lick their wounds. Rodgers went back to his flat and immediately wrote a song called 'F**k off!' Then he realized radio stations wouldn't be able to play it, so he changed the refrain to 'freak off!' and then, 'freak out!' Finally entitled 'Le Freak', the song shot straight to number one in the US and stayed there for seven weeks, selling over six million copies. His career took off, and from that moment on, the door to Studio 54 was always open to him. Rodgers' attitude to rejection sets him apart from most of us. He turned 'f**k off' into 'f**king brilliant'. He didn't bear a grudge, and the song lyrics even celebrated Studio 54.

Rejection is an alarm bell to wake you up and make you spring to action. Anger at rebuttal is a source of energy, and you can divert it to fuel your work. You learn more from a rebuff than from acceptance. You're forced to question what you're doing and whether it's worthwhile and if it is, you should throw everything at it. Rejection fires you up, so use the fire.

When Jeffrey Katzenberg was appointed head of production at Disney in the mid-80s, the company's reputation and profits were in freefall. He revitalized Disney's reputation and profits with *The Little Mermaid*, *Beauty and the Beast*, *Aladdin*, and *The Lion King*. He struck a deal to bring hugely successful Pixar, creators of *Toy Story* and *Finding Nemo*, on board. It was an astonishing turnaround. Everything was going well.

But then Katzenberg was suddenly fired after an argument with his boss, Michael Eisner. When you receive a knock, what counts is getting up the next day full of energy to fight on – intelligently. He won US$280 million in compensation and started a new company, DreamWorks SKG. It was a considerable risk; no one had set up a new Hollywood studio for sixty years. One of their first films, *Shrek*, ridiculed Disney's characters. In the film's opening scene we see Snow White and the Seven Dwarves, Pinocchio and Tinker Bell sold for rewards.

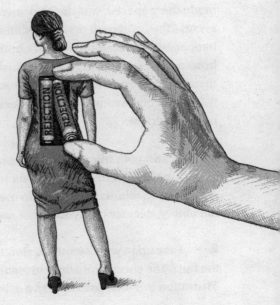

The city of Duloc mirrors Disneyland with the same castle towers – right down to the parking lots. The pompous Lord Farquaad (a joke on Lord F**k Wad) looks like a caricature of Michael Eisner.

There was no malice in Katzenberg's reaction; he was poking fun, showing that you can use rejection as a catapult to success. Katzenberg's rejection spurred him on to more significant achievements. Show the people who rejected you what they're missing. The history of art and of our own careers pivots on moments of rejection: how do we handle them? Do we act petulantly and tell ourselves we're right and our critics are wrong? Or do we re-examine our work with an open mind, ask ourselves what aspects we should rework? Criticism can be a launchpad if you use it correctly.

What was astonishing about Katzenberg and Rodgers, what made them special, was their positive attitude to negative events. They accepted that something unfortunate had happened and faced up to it with optimism. They worked out how to use their emotions in the most beneficial way. And their ability to recover made them successful, not dwelling on what had gone wrong but looking forward to how they could put things right.

1　　Adjust your mindset to think of rejection as an opportunity to learn. The successful turn the pain into self-growth; each rebuttal makes them more robust. Attitude, not ability, decides how you overcome failure.

2　　Face up to your emotions, don't suppress or deny the hurt. The successful admit to feeling humiliation and frustration but then use them as a driving force.

3   See rejection as evidence you're knocking on the door. The successful know rejection is an inevitable part of the process of getting somewhere. An open mind opens doors.

4   Don't let the fear of rejection stop you from having a go. When I was a student and applied to the Royal College of Art, I was so scared of being rejected that I produced masses of work. I poured everything I had into my portfolio and walked into the interview confident they'd accept me. They offered me a place, and that was my big break in life.

Acting 'as if'

Filippo Marinetti was desperate to be in the thick of things, but felt like he was stranded in a desert. In the early 1900s, Paris was the fiery centre where revolutionary new art movements like cubism and fauvism crashed into each other like tectonic plates. Artists, novelists and scientists sat together in cafés discussing new theories, and new young artists like Matisse, Picasso and Braque exploded onto the scene like volcanoes. But Marinetti was in Italy and felt overlooked. I know the feeling. I grew up in a small village in Wiltshire, England, with one bus an hour into the nearest small town. I knew I needed to be in London, but it felt like it was on another continent.

Marinetti published the Futurist Manifesto on the front page of the most influential newspaper in France, *Le Figaro*. It wasn't like a dry political manifesto; instead, it was full of passion and ideas. He declared futurism the shiny new 'ism' and mocked cubism as yesterday's movement: the subject of cubism was still lifes, landscapes and portraits – old, traditional formulas, but futurism was about the dynamism of the city; cars, trains and crowds rushing through city streets. Established artists like Picasso and Braque were outraged at this new volcano spraying lava over them. Marinetti rocketed from 'Who's he?' to 'Who does he think he is?'

Marinetti made sure everyone's telescope swung round to futurism. But he had a problem: futurism didn't exist. It was a manifesto without a movement. He had created a lot of gas and dust but he needed to pull it all together, and he put himself under tremendous pressure to deliver. He didn't sit on a good idea; he acted on it. He didn't go to a bank manager with a business plan or take the long, traditional route to acceptance. He quickly recruited like-minded artists to produce paintings and sculptures to embody futurist ideals. The futurist manifesto created a clear vision of the next step after cubism, and artists embraced his concept and wanted to be part of the following significant movement. The strategy worked, and Marinetti soon got his new 'ism' up and running – pick up an art history book and you'll find futurism, one of the significant art movements of the twentieth century. Marinetti proposed futurism – and then, crucially, created it. He stood up for what he believed in, attracted the eyes of the world, and then delivered the substance of his proposal.

Marinetti intuitively used a technique called 'acting as if', now used by psychologists, which is the result of research that proves if you act like the person you want to be then you will, in fact, become that person. Firstly, you have to find the attitude within you that's holding you back. Secondly, you need to establish the right motives. The goal is to change your inner self rather than change others' perceptions of you. If you try to look successful by wearing luxury brands, for example, research shows the technique fails and your self-worth decreases. Your aims have to be worthwhile and genuine for 'acting as if' to be effective.

A company was about to win a huge, game-changing contract from a client who ran the world's biggest internet search engine. But the client was worried they didn't have enough staff or resources and asked to visit their offices. The company called me to act as a creative consultant. The solution? Treble their team by asking friends and family in for the day to make the office look busy. They won the contract – then, with the money the new contract brought in, hired most of the people who had pretended to work there. Never promise what you can't deliver, but make promises that will stretch you.

1   What's the next step in your field? Marinetti worked out what was coming next in the art world, then produced it.

2   Declare your intentions – then fulfil them. 'Committing to a particular goal publicly puts pressure on oneself. It becomes an enormous action-forcing mechanism and often helps you achieve more than you might have done had you kept your goals to yourself,' said David Petraeus, former director of the CIA. 'Acting as if' means you'll have to learn the skills and find the ability to deliver. Put yourself in a position where you've got to come up with the goods. What would you do if you were confident? Bring your talents out into the open.

3   Only seek attention for the right reasons. Don't fake being something you're not, just to boost your ego. Commit to doing something worthwhile, honest and genuine.

'You have to be odd to be number one'

So said Dr Seuss, one of the most successful children's authors of all time. Wanting to do something brilliant makes you seem odd because you're sticking your neck out. Society wants you to stand in line and do what's acceptable – but 'acceptable' is never brilliant.

In the 1950s Dr Seuss hated the way children were taught to read with the mind-numbingly dull 'Dick and Jane' series of books – two normal children in a normal world doing normal things. Dick and Jane obeyed the rules and everything went smoothly in their lives. The books imposed an adult, sensible view of the world on children. Education authorities loved them, but children hated them.

Seuss wrote *The Cat in the Hat* in 1957 to make reading fun. It was anarchic, exuberant and free of moral lecturing, and there had never been a children's book like it. The cat was determined to make 'a cold, wet day' into a fun day. Dr Seuss wasn't afraid to write odd books about odd characters doing odd things, and he deliberately set out to write nonsense because it freed up his mind. He said, 'I like nonsense, it wakes up the brain cells.' His characters could go anywhere and do anything. Dr Seuss didn't look odd or behave strangely but he thought differently, and this was the key to the success of his books.

Several publishers rejected *The Cat in the Hat* for being too odd, but when he eventually found one prepared to take a risk, it was an instant hit. Seuss's books are still bestsellers because he tapped into the irreverent spirit of children. The safe 'Dick and Jane' books the authorities approved of are long forgotten. 'I have great pride in taking Dick and Jane out of most school libraries,' said Seuss. 'That is my greatest satisfaction.'

Hidden within his nonsense rhymes, though, was subversive advice to children. Dr Seuss found a release in nonsense: free your mind, was his approach. If you let go of logical thinking, you open your mind up to new ideas. You're free to do or say anything, instead of being trapped in the need to be taken seriously. 'Think left and think right and think low and think high. Oh the thinks you can think up if only you try!' Seuss's view was that you'll never be true to yourself if you worry what others think of you.

The art world didn't know how to categorize Yayoi Kusama. Her work was too unusual to fit into standard categories – was it pop art, op art, minimalist, environmental or what? She covered her paintings, drawings, sculptures and herself with dots, making her artwork and herself melt into the surroundings. She was about fun, polka dots and inflated shapes, but Kusama was also about decades of fighting prejudice against her mental condition (hallucinatory episodes), gender and ethnicity.

She used traditional media like paint on canvas, clothes, bags, jewellery, utensils, and furniture. It was her thinking that was odd and baffling to critics. It wasn't until she reached her eighties and nineties that a postmodern generation, uninterested in categories, appreciated her unique vision and responded directly to her work. She's now one of the most famous artists globally, with retrospectives in every major gallery in the world – in 2018 alone her work made over $108 million in total at auction.

1 See the label of 'odd' as a badge of honour. If you're doing something completely new, people will think it's odd. Dare to be different. But don't expect support from friends, family and colleagues. They'll have their own reasons for wanting you to conform.

2 Be 'Youer than You!' People will always be resentful if you take a risk where they played safe. A lot of people I was at school with wanted to be artists, but they took the easy route and took conventional jobs. By the time they were in their late thirties and forties they felt empty, as if they had wasted their youth. I went to art college, got into the RCA and had a successful one-man show and received glowing reviews in the press. It annoyed them. It made them feel even worse about the choices they had made.

3 Don't expect your close friends and family to like it if you follow your own interests. Like Seuss and Kusama, you'll have to put up with getting kicked around and work ten times harder than those taking the safe route because you'll have more hurdles to jump. But the reward of being your true self rather than a reproduction of what society wants makes it all worth it.

The power of outsider thinking

Do you ever feel like an outsider, like the people in power have shut you out and continuously put obstacles in your way?

Feeling like an outsider does not mean there's something wrong with you. An outsider is not a strange person without friends; they just have different values and a different perspective. It's an advantage to look at the world from outside: an insider adopts the accepted standards, but outsiders question what is blindly accepted. If you see things differently, help others to see things from your perspective.

The education system teaches you to think conventionally, but brilliant work is always unconventional. There is huge pressure on us to get academic qualifications and merge into the system. People who produce excellent work were sometimes underachievers at school or university; they were impatient with being lectured at, memorizing facts and then regurgitating them. Their instinct is to act – to get out there and make stuff. The skill they don't teach you at school is how to think for yourself, but the self-taught produce fresh, innovative work because they find their own, new methods. When someone says, 'It's not the done thing,' do it and then it will become the done thing.

Everything was against Eileen Gray. In the 1920s, you needed strict qualifications to become an architect but entry to academic courses was strictly controlled by men. Gray refused

to accept the cards she'd been dealt – no one was going to help her, so she helped herself, rolled up her sleeves, picked up a hammer and nails and made her vision a reality. The tough situation brought out the innovator in her and she taught herself all the skills an architect needed from books and evening classes. She realized that other architects' work was predictable because they were insiders keeping to the design rules of the profession, and the big architecture firms repeated the same old designs and practices, but she could do things differently and stand out.

Gray didn't study architecture at university – she learned for herself by making groundbreaking buildings and furniture. She taught herself whatever skills she needed: leadership, mathematics, legal skills, architectural drawing, electrical home wiring, engineering, and more. What we produce must be structurally sound but reflect our own unique vision, and Gray went down in the history of design as a pioneer of the

Modern Movement because her unique working process stood out from the trained architects. She started by making chairs and tables. Gray's Occasional Table, designed in 1927, is still a bestseller because it embodies her unique attitude and principles. She used the latest materials, a tubular steel base and glass top, to create a multipurpose and adjustable table that was both modern and classic. No one could question whether Gray's ideas would work because the proof was in front of their eyes – she made them with her own hands. They existed. She proved that when the insiders are ganging up against you, the solution is to act – use your energy and enthusiasm to transform a bad situation into a good one. Her furniture and her architecture became significant because it was new, different, and reflected her feminine, free-flowing, instinctive attitude.

Imagine someone with no training building a house from scratch: attracting the finance, producing detailed plans of electrical circuits, plumbing, structural stresses and then actually building it. It shows us all what is possible if we put our minds to it. In 1926, Gray began building a house near Monaco. A foreigner in France couldn't own property, so she bought a cheap scrap of rocky land and put it in her partner's name. The house, enigmatically called E-1027, was a white beacon of enlightenment, jutting out on pillars from jagged rocks, with huge horizontal windows and an open facade. E-1027 immediately attracted international recognition as a masterpiece and commissions flooded in.

Gray sold the house and moved on to other projects, but her success annoyed architects who had spent years studying at university and working as apprentices. She showed them you don't have to rely on established structures; instead you can think and work for yourself. The great architect Le Corbusier admired E-1027 and frequently stayed there in order to study and learn from it. But he was also jealous and resentful, and in 1938 he vandalized the walls with cubist murals of naked women, deliberately violating Gray's express instructions that E-1027 must be left free of any decoration. Architecture critic Rowan Moore called it a man asserting 'his dominion, like a urinating dog, over the territory'. Gray's confidence to think and act independently infuriated the architecture establishment.

Resist the desire to be an insider. As an outsider you'll have to make it with your own hands in your own way. Gray's legacy reassures us that if you work hard, with your own hands and your own ideas, you can do it with more pride and do it better than anyone else. Truthfully, Gray wanted to be an insider, she wanted to be accepted by the world of architecture, and ultimately she achieved her goal. But coming at it from the outside made her distinctive. Many creative outsiders have been offered knighthoods by the British establishment when they've proved themselves – Francis Bacon, David Bowie, L. S. Lowry, Henry Moore, Joseph Conrad, Michael Faraday, David Hockney – only to decline them because they didn't want to lose their outsider perspective. Bob Dylan hesitated before accepting the Nobel Prize when he was seventy-five. It was a great honour, but he struggled for months before finally accepting.

We all want to feel comfortable, accepted, and a member of the club. But you have to fight against your desire for approval. Significant advances in literature, music or science are produced by outsiders, and only an outsider can make revolutionary changes. They don't constantly look over their shoulder and worry about being thrown out of the club, because they aren't in one.

1   Learn by doing because your best teacher is experience. You're the best teacher of yourself, because you understand yourself better than anyone else. If you're thoroughly dedicated and study something deeply, you can teach yourself whatever you need to know. Gray worked phenomenally hard, and she was on the site of E-1027 every day for three years. Find your unique way of working. Because it's original, it will have more impact.

2   If you don't know how to do something, don't automatically seek instruction – work it out for yourself first. By finding out for yourself, you can question things as you progress, and it'll make your work stand out more. Using other people's thinking is more comfortable, but it's lazy. As a university tutor, I show students how to think for themselves and be independent. I encourage them to unlearn everything they learned at school.

3   Adopt an outsider attitude. The insider is a cog in a machine, but an outsider creates their own machine. Outsiders are comfortable with new ideas. Because outsiders are true to themselves, they rarely look back and wish they had done things differently. Outsiders are more committed to their work than to gaining approval, and more fulfilled because they listen to their inner voice and follow their intuition. Gray found the life of an outsider challenging, but ultimately more worthwhile.

Look closer. See deeper. Achieve more

Where do you start if you haven't got an extraordinary, transformative idea? Well, if you wait until that moment then you could be sitting around forever. Don't set out to create a revolutionary breakthrough, because you're putting yourself under enormous pressure and could freeze. Start with a small idea, then develop it into something big. Create something new by making minor improvements to something that already exists. Work out how to push it forwards. The beauty of this method is that you only have to take small steps and eventually, many small developments will combine to create a new, groundbreaking revolution.

The history of any field is one of incremental developments – not giant leaps. Take the telephone: when the iPhone was launched, everyone thought it was a big, new idea, but actually it was a slow evolution. There was no eureka moment. The iPhone took years to come into existence – you could argue it took 150 years, from the moment the telephone was first invented. Apple's 'historic breakthrough' came from many small improvements to inventions that already existed: FingerWorks pioneered touchscreen technology. Samsung claimed Apple was inspired by its pinch and zoom feature after they introduced it to some Apple engineers. Fujitsu built a touchscreen device called the iPAD a decade before Apple. The list of influences goes on and on . . . But Apple's genius was to add other inventions and improve them until the final result was the brilliant iPhone.

In 1676, Isaac Newton wrote in a letter to his rival Robert Hooke, 'If I have seen a little further it is by standing on the shoulders of Giants.' He was acknowledging that he'd used the knowledge gained by previous scientists, then pushed it forwards little by little until he'd made a radical breakthrough. People who make a massive contribution to science, art or business know they were able to see a little further because of those who preceded them.

When I am a creative consultant to hospitals, I ask the surgeons and doctors to adopt the 'improvement' mindset. After a procedure, for example an operation, we assess every aspect to analyse how the surgical instruments could be improved, then the preparation, process or communication within the team. This has resulted in many new ideas. An artificial liver is a huge, heavy piece of equipment mounted on a trolley (imagine a wayward supermarket trolley with half a ton of metal in it). Tired patients had to push it around by hand while connected to it with tubes and wires. We applied the improvement technique and eventually created the concept of an artificial liver mounted on a buggy that patients could sit in and drive around with ease. We pushed it to be as good as it could be. Take things as far as they can go. Keep asking yourself: is this the best possible version?

A colossal goal can seem daunting and overwhelming, such as an epic novel, a feature film, or a one-person exhibition. Start by asking, what small win can I achieve today? You'll find yourself moving forward and picking up speed as you go. Duty seems like an old-fashioned concept, but you have an obligation to yourself and to your work to make it as amazing as possible.

1   Find the work you admire and investigate it for untapped potential. Remake it and add as many improvements as you can. This will transform it into your personal work featuring your concerns and interests.

2   Ask questions. What could be bigger, smaller or more interactive? What if you changed the materials into more unusual and unexpected substances? Could you make it more dynamic – make something static move?

3   Continuous transformation is essential for successful innovation. Adopt the mindset of constant growth – there is always space for improvement. Never sit back on your laurels or you'll miss opportunities, and don't assume yesterday's success will still be a triumph tomorrow.

Like something everyone else hates

When Yale University professors Denise Scott Brown and
Robert Venturi slipped into a casino in Las Vegas in 1968,
the two academics were out of place among the high rollers
with Rolex watches, crocodile-skin shoes and orange fake
tans. Scott Brown and Venturi were there to gamble.
It paid off big time for them, but their method can
work for you too.

Most projects require research. Look in the usual places,
books, the internet or museums, and you'll find the typical
answers. But how can you research creatively? Live research
is observing something in real life. Look in unusual places,
and you'll discover unexpected inspiration. The architecture
professors were looking in a casino for new ideas – and you'll
be surprised by what they found, and how they used it to boost
their careers.

In the 1960s, students learned the principles of architecture
by worshipping Ludwig Mies van der Rohe, Walter Gropius,
and their acolytes. The strict modernist rules were: no
ornamentation; everything must have a function; no colours,
only grey or white. Structures must be pure, uncluttered
geometric shapes like rectangles. The only approved materials
were reinforced concrete and steel. Mies van der Rohe hated
tenants in his buildings having curtains of different colours
and opening them to different widths, so he installed blinds
that only worked in three positions: fully open, half drawn, or

fully drawn. Tenants hated living in modernist buildings, but they had no choice.

What modernist architects hated most was Las Vegas. For them, it was hell on earth, the antithesis of modernism – a cluttered, commercialized strip of unplanned casinos and bars plastered in scrolling video screens, vulgar kitsch and pulsing neon signs. Girls, girls, girls! Casino! Jackpot frenzy! Show time! Get rich quick! Win a million! Sin City was devoted to hedonism, the result of giving money and popular taste free rein. Everything about it insulted and upset middle-class, academic and intellectual values.

Venturi and Scott Brown decided to outrage modernists by taking their architecture students to study Las Vegas. In the spirit of gambling, they played a game of 'I bet I can like something worse than you can like' and called it 'hate–love exhilaration'. There was a sense of freedom to throwing away established good taste and deliberately liking the garish bling,

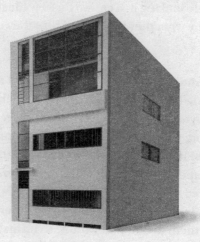

Less is a bore

and they discovered unexpected value in the forbidden jungle of trashy, chaotic buildings. Venturi explained his ideas in the successful book *Learning from Las Vegas*. He electrified the austere world of architectural philosophy by opening up a new range of possibilities, and turned against modernist principles he now saw as sterile and vacuous, famously declaring 'less is bore' (the saying 'less is more' having been coined by humourless Mies van der Rohe). Suddenly anything was possible. Buildings could mix popular styles from Greek, Roman or anywhere. Venturi attacked good taste because it imposed restrictive rules, and went down in the history of architecture for sparking the postmodern movement. Viva Las Vegas!

Venturi and Scott Brown's game, 'I bet I can like something worse than you can like', led to remarkable new insights and ideas. It's a game you too should play every day in order to question accepted standards and see the value in the derided and unfashionable. It's about interrogating the rules imposed

More is . . .

on us in our sphere. Venturi understood that modernist architecture began with good intentions, to create a utopian society. But it led to austere, puritanical buildings of glass and steel. Mies van der Rohe believed everyone must live a severe and regimented life, so his buildings and interiors were designed with the austerity of a church. 'There is no reason that a cathedral should not be built to the same architectural standards as a garage,' Mies said. He created the Illinois Institute of Technology's chapel, nicknamed the 'God box' because it could have been a garage or a storage depot. Be open to liking what everyone else hates; it opens doors in your mind.

Artist Grayson Perry's secular chapel, A House for Essex, is exuberant and thoughtful, the embodiment of Venturi's idea of mixing different styles or content together. It's a demonstration of the benefit of working without restrictive rules and conventions shackling your mind, an emotional mixture of church, Asian temple and fairy-tale cottage. Plastered with coloured tiles showing images that tell the life story of Julie, a fictional Essex woman, the house is covered in small sculptures mimicking pagan fertility symbols. It's hugely popular with the public.

Steven Tyler plays a strange game called 'Dare to Suck'. Once a week, he calls his rock band, Aerosmith, together, and each member must present an idea they think is embarrassing and awful. Usually it is, but every now and then, it produces a classic track. Tyler releases the band's inhibitions by starting with something embarrassing; the ideas can only get better from here. When I'm working with students or as a consultant, my first step is to get people to overcome this fear of embarrassing themselves.

'Good taste is death; vulgarity is life,' said designer Mary Quant. Good taste is restrictive; you're pinned down by the opinions of others. If you are prepared to embrace bad taste, you're set free. Good taste makes you a slave to the opinions of others – if you're dependent on their approval, you are in prison, and if you're not careful, you are led by their views more than yours. The great pop artist Roy Lichtenstein said he painted blown-up details of popular, trashy comic strips to annoy the art establishment. Jeff Koons scaled up garish tourist souvenirs into massive sculptures so the art elite would be forced to look at the trash they avoided. What distinguishes James Dyson, Elon Musk, Richard Branson and all groundbreaking entrepreneurs is their irreverent attitude to standard values. It freed them up. They no longer had to worry whether people thought their work was tasteful or high class. Be prepared to be vulgar. Using what everyone has dismissed as trashy and worthless is a way of pulling down hierarchies and challenging established values. It's good to be liked by others, but it's important not to become dependent on their approval.

1   Play the game 'I bet I can like something worse than you can like'. Step off the road approved by the elite of your field, and you're in unexplored territory. Search for inspiration in the derided and ridiculed areas *because* they're derided and ridiculed. Discover and celebrate their overlooked qualities.

2   Be aware of your selective thinking. We all automatically approve of some values and dismiss others. We find ourselves believing conventional values when there is no proof. Could whatever makes something 'bad' actually be what's 'good' about it? Examine and question your assumptions about why you think something is 'bad'.

3   When you find 'something worse', investigate its 'worseness'. Throw yourself into it – enjoy and celebrate the freedom to explore the ridiculed.

Be the first to the future

Are you stuck for an idea? Go back to the future and steal a great one from the past. No copyright problems! Find someone from the past who you identify with and whose work had an impact. Put yourself in their shoes and remake their work for modern times.

For decades, Hollywood made clichéd gangster movies with choreographed and meticulously planned fight scenes. An unknown film director wanted his low-budget gangster movie to be gritty and real, so he turned to Caravaggio, a seventeenth-century painter. At that time, the convention was for paintings to show religious figures like saints and disciples as otherworldly and ethereal – even though they were poor carpenters, fishermen, tax collectors and thieves, who had led a hard life but triumphed over adversity. Instead of using professional models, Caravaggio asked low-life criminals and prostitutes to pose for him. He didn't hide their dirty fingernails and filthy feet. In paintings like *The Calling of St Matthew*, a biblical story was made vividly real by setting it in a gritty ghetto. The realism caused outrage in the Catholic Church, but the public could relate to the figures for the first time.

The young director was Martin Scorsese, and he copied Caravaggio's realism in his film *Mean Streets*. He said the bar scene was '*The Calling of St Matthew* but in New York. Making films with street people was what it was really about, like [Caravaggio] made paintings with them.' Scorsese kept to Caravaggio's realist approach throughout the film, using unknown actors like Robert de Niro and Harvey Keitel, who the audience wouldn't recognize. The fight scenes looked real because they were unplanned and not staged like Hollywood fights. The cameraman shot in a documentary style with a handheld camera and had to scramble over furniture because he had no idea where the actors would go as they fought. He captured the wild, unpredictable action. When a drunk character lurched around a party, Scorsese caught the unsteady feeling by strapping a camera to the actor's head as he swayed around. Characters talked over each other, just like people do in real-life conversations.

Caravaggio's characters loomed out of extreme contrasts of dark and light, and Scorsese copied the effect to emphasize the seedy drama of the backstreets. 'There was no doubt it could be taken into cinema because of the use of light and shadow, the chiaroscuro effect,' said Scorsese. If Caravaggio had been alive in the 1970s, he would have made *Mean Streets*. Scorsese didn't just copy Caravaggio's style but also his intentions – to be as real as possible. Audiences were shocked by the raw, harsh realities of this truly original form of filmmaking; it seemed radically new and fresh in 1973 and was an instant success.

Everyone knows who you've copied if your source is the latest sensation in your field. Most filmmakers are influenced by a film that came out six months earlier or something they saw on TV the previous night, or Netflix, or a music video on YouTube. Instead, copy from a source everyone has forgotten but was once great. If Scorsese had copied, say, Orson Welles or Brian de Palma, we'd have recognized the style. He leaned on another artist, but the film critics and audience didn't know who.

1   Who is your Caravaggio? If you want to shock your audience with a radical, fresh new idea they've never seen before, search in a national gallery, classical music, or a medieval book, and no one will know your source. Find work that strikes a chord with you. If something has lasted hundreds of years, it's persisted for a reason. Take brilliant but forgotten ideas from the past and make them new and relevant.

2   Transfer the timeless quality that exists in a Caravaggio, or whatever you choose, and it will ensure your work will last. Caravaggio's work lasts because it touches on the core of what it is to be human. Perennial successes like Harry Potter, Tintin or *Star Wars* have everlasting themes based on the 'hero myth'.

3   If a musician picks up themes used by Mozart instead of whatever is top of the dance charts today, it could be modern, radical and challenging (like Mozart) but also timeless (like Mozart). Ask yourself if what you're doing will still be relevant in a decade.

Hyperfocus in a world of interruption

Our attention is distracted by the chaos of modern life. Writer Linda Stone worked as an executive for Apple and researcher for Microsoft and was the person who coined the term continuous partial attention. CPA is always on, anywhere, anytime, behaviour. Our eyes flick around but never give full attention to something. We are lured off course by our culture pummelling us with quick, short bites of information. Hyperfocus, on the other hand, keeps you to the best course of action.

Hyperfocus is noticing what happens around us and deciding what deserves our attention. Our focus is a source of strength if we direct it properly, but a weakness if we point it in the wrong direction. It takes self-discipline to filter and choose from the overwhelming information submerging us, but your attention is a precious resource. Let others be easily distracted, but to create brilliant work, you must focus only on what is essential.

A distinguishing feature of all the great artists from Constable to Warhol was their ability to focus relentlessly on what mattered. Great writers like Hemingway and Virginia Woolf developed hyperfocus by always watching and making notes on everyone and everything around them. Musicians like Lady Gaga and Björk pick up sounds and ideas from the street. Their switch is constantly 'on'. They are always watching and searching.

For years, the University of Maryland football players wore heavy shirts under their outer padding (or 'armour') during games, and they quickly became soaked in sweat. One player, Kevin Plank, found it a real problem, so he focused on creating an undershirt designed to stay dry during even the most energetic games. It was so effective that other players in his team wanted one, and then word spread to others. He started manufacturing them, and in 1997 drove around the east coast selling from his car. He called his company Under Armour. Last time I looked, it had over US$4 billion in annual revenues. When Plank saw there was a glimmer of potential in Under Armour, he directed all his attention towards its development. Nothing distracted him. Hyperfocus requires you to deprive yourself of TV, leisure, partying or anything that doesn't help your project. There's a saying, 'All work and no play makes Jack a dull boy'. But for successful artists, scientists and entrepreneurs, their work is also their play. For them, there is nothing more fun than working on their project.

Direct your attention like a camera lens onto what matters – then bring it into sharp focus. Your most powerful resource is your concentration, but most of us are busy squandering it on the irrelevant. With focus, you'll get stuff done and be more fulfilled.

In 2002, Father Bernard McCoy couldn't find a cheap replacement for his ink cartridge when his printer ran dry. He discovered it was easy to source the pigment from suppliers and fill the cartridges himself. So why not do it for others? In between pumping out Gregorian chants in the monastery of the Cistercian Abbey in Monroe County, Wisconsin, he started an ink cartridge-refilling business with the other brothers. The company, LaserMonks Inc., was soon producing hundreds of

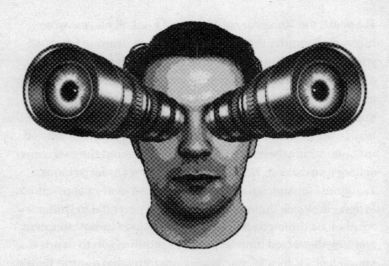

thousands of dollars for their charity. Problem-solving is an
important attribute, but finding problems to solve is an even
more critical talent to nurture. It's a skill that requires you
to be alert, always on the lookout for opportunity. It wasn't
an accident that he was a monk; he was used to tuning out
external distractions and using mindfulness to develop higher
concentration. The ability to ignore the noise of the modern
world helped him to focus.

Hyperfocus is the art of maintaining attention; it takes self-
discipline to ignore the noise and look intensely. We solve
problems every day but don't notice they could be significant.
Solving a micro-problem often leads to a macro-solution, and
hyperfocus is about seeing opportunities in the minutiae other
people miss.

You might look around and feel nothing unusual is going
on – but it is. When you have a camera and take photos, you
become more aware of your surroundings. You notice things

you wouldn't usually see. Nick Cave's book *The Sick Bag Song* came from observations travelling in planes during a US concert tour. With a camera, you scan the world for exciting things – people, angles – and you pay a lot more attention to what's around you. It changes your thinking, opens your eyes. You need to be just as focused when you haven't got a camera.

In the early twentieth century, most haircare products targeted at African American women were produced by white-owned companies who didn't have a good understanding of the specific haircare needs of black women. As an African American woman, Madam C. J. Walker felt ignored – so she invented products targeted at women like her. She became one of the most successful businesswomen of all time and is widely considered America's first self-made female millionaire. For an African American woman to make headway in the business world in those times required an extraordinary effort, so to develop her business, she learned to live with less: less leisure time, fewer distractions and fewer holidays. Innumerable hurdles were in front of her, and she needed hyperfocus to leap over all of them.

Focus on where you can be most effective and what you can control. The ability to direct yourself is your main asset. What you choose to do and where you direct your energy is your choice and all-important, so point the spotlight on something you can solve and be prepared to say 'no' so that you can say 'yes' to what is essential. Focus on actions, on actually doing something.

1   If you hyperfocus in a blurred world, you'll have an advantage. Focus on taking small steps towards a big goal. We live in a world where things appear and disappear with speed;

everything is moving, so don't let your attention become fuzzy. Multitasking has a cognitive penalty: research has proved that multitaskers make more mistakes and take longer than if they'd focused on one thing at a time. In tests, people who thought they were good at multitasking actually performed the worst.

2 Edit out distractions. Remove anything from your attention that distracts you from producing something brilliant. The successful people I've met aren't busy. They aren't talking on the phone non-stop, rushing here and there to appointments, popping in and out of meetings. They're hyperfocused. Some people need to look busy so others think they're in demand. It makes them feel emotionally satisfied, but they don't advance towards their goals. The hyperfocused make definite steps towards what is important to them. Sometimes they sit and think and mull over a problem and aren't busy for long periods. A frantic lifestyle is not the same as being productive.

3 Build your willpower. Attention strengthens your willpower because you have to stay hyperfocused on the task at hand. You are not distracted and you channel all your energy into completing your goal.

Ha + ha = aha

Work is a serious business. Our livelihoods depend on being successful, and we want our colleagues and organizations to see we take our work seriously. If something matters to us, we become earnest and concerned. Our thinking becomes narrow, tight, and restricted. But significant advances come from minds that are open, adventurous and free of restraints.

If you want to produce great work, you need to develop the ability to be simultaneously deeply serious and light-hearted. Many great artworks, businesses, songs and novels began as a joke. Mark Zuckerberg said Facebook began as a joke: 'It all started with the dream of helping people keep track of how fat their exes have gotten.' One of rock band Blur's biggest hits, 'Song 2', was a joke, according to band member Graham Coxon. It was presented to the record company executives as a prank, mock-grunge single to 'blow the . . . labels' heads off'. But it was the executives who shocked the band by approving it as their next release. Writer Ottessa Moshfegh bought a book on how to write a novel in 90 days. She said attempting to do it herself started out as a joke, but then grew into something more serious. *Eileen* won literary awards and was nominated for the Booker Prize.

Researchers have discovered that humour activates the brain's limbic system and connects activity from the right and left sides; the frontal lobe, used for judgment, turns off when fooling around and joking. Sigmund Freud took jokes seriously. He was the first to notice the connection between humour, the subconscious and innovation. In his book *The Joke and Its Relation to the Unconscious*, Freud argued that humour, like dreams, gives us pleasure by releasing our inhibitions and letting us express subversive, playful or unusual ideas that we usually hide. Humour leads to the conceptual elasticity essential for creative thinking; when you joke, your internal critic shrinks away, allowing unique ideas to dance freely. Ha ha creates more aha. Being judgmental is useful when you've produced something, but not during the process.

When Meret Oppenheim had coffee in a Paris café with Pablo Picasso in 1936, he noticed her metal bracelet was covered in fur and joked you could cover anything with fur, 'even this cup and saucer'. He called to the waiter, 'More fur!' Immediately after the meeting, Oppenheim bought a teacup, saucer and spoon, covered them in fur, and titled the sculpture *Le Déjeuner en fourrure*. To Oppenheim, it was an absurd joke. Her friends found it hilarious, so when she exhibited the small object, she was surprised when the public and critics reacted with horror and outrage. She didn't expect a joke to be taken seriously and find its way into important art history books. Her sculpture is the quintessential surrealist object – something mundane changed in an unexpected way to challenge reason. Buoyed by the success of her teacup, Oppenheim used Freud's ideas to deliberately produce work generated not from the conscious (the cerebral, restricted area of the brain), but the unconscious (the absurd, dreaming, irrational area).

Steve Jobs averaged one joke a minute during his iconic keynote speech to launch the iPhone – more than most stand-up comedians. Being solemn doesn't make you better at what you do, it makes you worse. You need the right and left sides of your mind working in tandem. Research by psychologists has shown that top executives joke twice as often as middle-ranking executives. The funnier they are, the more successful they become.

My father spent his life flying aeroplanes in the RAF. It surprised me how even in life and death situations, he and his colleagues still cracked jokes. Being jovial stopped them panicking and freezing up and helped them stay calm and focused – a more conducive state for problem-solving than being grim and worried. If they could be light-hearted in life and death situations, anyone can. If a significant problem developed with an engine, they were still joking even in the face of potential disaster. Being humourless is easy; keeping a sense of humour in a tense situation is much harder. Research has demonstrated that people who use humour switch from convergent thinking, where they have a single answer, to divergent thinking, where they have numerous ideas.

1   If you are absorbed in a problem, you can take it so seriously your mind becomes restricted. Consciously try to be simultaneously serious and playful. The ideas will flow more naturally.

2   Important work and instances of great drama juxtapose moments of humour with tragedy. The contrast creates friction and energy. Work with it and use the vigour to your advantage.

Generate opportunities

There are three types of people. Those who miss opportunities. Those who grasp opportunities. And those who generate them.

We miss opportunities because we convince ourselves we're not fully prepared, lack the skills, or it's not the right moment – but you're never ready for a significant performance, exhibition, exam or pitch. You could always have practised more, studied more, or researched more thoroughly. Jump in even when you're not ready. Do things before you know how to do them. If you don't take the opportunity, you'll end up working for someone who did.

The major fashion house Gucci had been top of the fashion world for decades, but it slowly went into decline. Sales were still billions of dollars a year, but profits were plummeting. Gucci had become lethargic, so in 2014, a new CEO, Marco Bizzarri, decided to appoint a new chief designer to turn things around. The standard practice was to play safe and sign up a star designer with an impressive track record to give the public confidence, but first, Bizzarri interviewed Gucci backroom staff for their views. Accessories designer Alessandro Michele impressed him with exciting suggestions, so Bizzarri gambled and offered Michele the job with a proposition that's become a fashion legend: he asked Michele to redesign and reimagine the label for a new collection – a task that usually took months of intense preparation – in just five days. 'It was a way for me to see if

Alessandro was willing to take risks,' said Bizzarri. 'Because considering the kind of turnaround that I had in mind, I needed a person who was willing, like me, to take big risks – and maybe make big mistakes. If he was going to tell me no, then I didn't want to be with someone who was risk-averse.' Gucci was a multimillion-dollar business, but Bizzarri urged Michele to make an extreme statement – no matter how uncommercial. And he succeeded: within the week, Michele had a collection of thirty-six outfits finished and ready for a catwalk show.

Sometimes we find ourselves in situations where we have to convince ourselves we have what it takes and we're up to the task. The feeling we can't do something is an obstacle we place in front of our success. You create or destroy your progress, depending on how you see yourself, but your perceptions are within your control and it's down to you whether you go for it or not.

Feverish anticipation greeted Michele's debut because he went for eccentric, eclectic designs. The press admired the way he used fashion as an agent for change with gender-fluid designs. Michele went on to dissolve polarized boundaries, with female models wearing the men's collection and vice versa; he reinvented Gucci with a radical new vision and Gucci became the leading fashion brand. Everything stemmed from grasping the one opportunity he was offered and creating more openings.

1   If you're offered a great opportunity but are unsure if you're up to the task, say 'yes' and then find a way to deliver. No one is ever ready for the big breaks. They only arrive a few times in your life – seize them.

2   Don't fear taking risks – fear playing safe. If you take a chance and fail, at least you tried. If you play safe, you'll never know what might have happened. Don't put barriers in the way of your success. Most people think they want a breakthrough, but they find reasons why they can't take it when it arrives.

3   You do your best work when your back is against the wall. You can always find a pathway. But you'll have to make it.

Throw away the map.
Follow a compass

It's a waste of time making career plans and mapping out organizational strategies in detail. A map is useful on stable, charted land, but our new globalized world is complex, ever-changing and unpredictable. With a rigid plan, when something goes unexpectedly wrong, it snaps. What should your tactics be in a world where strategy is outdated? Think compass, not map. Have a destination in mind, but don't follow a route; with a compass, you can keep all your options open and be flexible. The upside of an age of uncertainty is that it is fertile ground for unexpected opportunities.

Artist Faith Ringgold had a compass, and the needle pointed to civil rights, but as a woman of colour she had to adapt to circumstances. During her early life, while producing art, Ringgold taught in schools and universities, and she also wrote and illustrated seventeen children's books. She achieved greater recognition year by year, through her forties and fifties, and she fed every experience back into her work.

Ringgold is an excellent example of what psychologists define as 'adversarial growth'. Each setback seemed to strengthen her; she learned from it and used it. Research by sports psychologist David Fletcher of Loughborough University has proved that the ability to adapt to unplanned changes, such as a severe injury, is crucial to recovery. The world's best athletes benefit from traumatic adversity. 'At the highest level of competition, phenomenal levels of psychological resilience are necessary to attain and sustain success,' Fletcher noted. He also noticed that athletes became more resilient after a devastating injury, and their performance improved. The world's best athletes display 'adversarial growth', adapting to severe injuries or setbacks, such as being dropped from the team. Sports coaches actively help athletes develop adversarial growth, which can be used by anyone in any profession. When Ringgold's work didn't go as well as she'd planned, she took trips to Europe and Africa, picked up new influences, and her work took off in different directions. Ringgold switched from painting to the more humble medium of quilts after visiting the Rijksmuseum, Amsterdam, and seeing a collection of Nepali artwork. It was a breakthrough moment for her, because quilts are now her signature medium. She didn't gain worldwide recognition until she was in her seventies and eighties, when she finally emerged as an influential contemporary artist.

'Adversarial growth' is something we can nurture. Limor Fried began a do-it-yourself electronics e-commerce company, Adafruit, when she was still a student at MIT. She didn't have any detailed business plan, but she saw the potential in online sales of DIY kits of replica *Space Invaders* cabinets, assembling the kits using off-the-shelf parts available to anyone from online electronics stores. She used the compass mindset, and customers were thrilled by her kits.

No one gave you a script for your life. You have no choice but to improvise, respond to an ever-changing world, and point yourself in the direction of your compass needle. Due to clever merchandising, Adafruit soon had a hundred employees and profits of millions a year. As with Wrigley, the key to Fried's success was an adaptable frame of mind. She set off in a direction and worked things out as she went along, and this kind of flexible thinking is an example to us all: start something, see what happens and decide what to throw out or keep. We discover by trying things out and seeing what works. It's essential to be adaptable and accept there is no one right path. The successful don't sit around planning, they get on with it, and improvise with whatever arises and whatever resources they have – no matter how sparse.

Ingvar Kamprad started a small mail-order business selling Christmas cards. Then he began selling folders and pens. Later, he added furniture designed by local craftsmen. His business snowballed, and other furniture manufacturers feared his rapid growth, so they banned him from trade shows. He hired a large warehouse in the countryside and filled it with his furniture for customers to view before they ordered them. One day Kamprad noticed that an employee about to deliver a table couldn't fit it into the boot of their car, so they unscrewed the legs. Kamprad liked the idea of customers assembling the furniture themselves, and it proved to be popular. The big furniture stores attacked again, banning established designers from working for him, so he had to hire young, inexperienced designers. But there was an unexpected benefit to this, since they had newer, more adventurous ideas. Once more the big furniture stores attacked, and banned wood merchants from supplying him. He had to source wood from Poland. But in doing so, he discovered better quality wood at half the price, and he could undercut the big companies. When Kamprad opened his first, mega, flagship IKEA store in 1965, there was a huge crowd. The manager panicked and let the customers go directly to the warehouse at the back of the store to find the furniture, and Kamprad decided to keep this feature – self-service warehouses. In 2020 IKEA made £50 billion in sales to over a billion visitors. Kamprad is a perfect example of 'adversarial growth': every knock built him up. He used unplanned adversity to improve IKEA.

1   Don't make detailed plans. How often have you heard *When I have more money, I'll do something brilliant* or *When I can afford a studio* . . . ? Follow a map, and you'll get stuck on the same old pathways. Set out with a compass and aim yourself at a destination. Be flexible about what route you take.

2   Set off with a direction and a vision of your end goal. Produce brilliant work by getting on with it and using whatever abilities and materials are available to you.

3   Use 'adversarial growth'. Be flexible: go around, underneath and over obstacles. People become standardized because they follow the routes laid out for them. They attend similar university courses, read identical books, watch the same TV programmes and use the same old internet sources. If you don't have the right credentials, be successful by learning from adversity.

Be a creativity magnet

Many workplaces are sterile. They may be efficient and well organized, but they stifle and suffocate. Even an artist must refresh their studio frequently, or it becomes limiting.

You have to create an effective workplace deliberately. Make a creative environment for others and yourself, because your workplace either helps to push you towards your goal or it holds you back. And try to craft it to your needs; you need to feel free to experiment and explore openly to produce brilliant work.

Florence Knoll was a successful designer and architect in her own right before co-founding Knoll Studio. She elevated furniture design and manufacture to a higher level than had ever been seen. But to keep coming up with exciting new designs year after year was challenging. She was always looking for new ways to get great ideas, so she decided to try a radical approach.

Instead of hiring a new designer, which would have been the usual course of action, Knoll studio gave sculptor Harry Bertoia space in their factory, but didn't ask him to design furniture. Instead they encouraged him to make sculptures and 3D forms, and if he produced something interesting, let them see. Sculptors often used wire netting as a base for plaster or clay, and Bertoia saw that a chair was just a sculpture – but one you could sit on. To Knoll's surprise, in 1952 Bertoia produced one of the most iconic and most significant triumphs of twentieth-century design – the Diamond Chair. Bertoia said of the wire chairs, 'They are mainly made of air, like sculpture. Space passes right through them.' Knoll got the best out of him by trusting him and giving him freedom. The chair was his most brilliant achievement (better than his sculptures) and assured him a place in the history of design.

As a university tutor and consultant for businesses, creating an atmosphere where people feel confident to propose crazy ideas, fail and look silly is one of my most important tasks. It is human nature to worry about what other people think of you, and creating an environment where people feel free is harder than it seems. People are more affected by their environment than their work routines. Stanford psychologist and behaviourist B. J. Fogg says the working environment's design is more important than willpower, because work environments are designed to create distraction and interruption, not for people to become absorbed in their work.

Artist Martin Kippenberger refused to teach in the university studios where he was employed as a tutor, because students adopted a 'university mentality' while there. Instead, he held tutorials in cafés and bars where he and his students stopped playing the role of student and teacher. In an academic atmosphere, students became 'academic' and used university jargon. In a café, they spoke about their work in real-world terms. He was conscious of how the environment affected the students' thinking, and he wanted them to think openly – not like university students.

1   Don't let your studio or office just happen, actively create it – and don't think of it as a studio or office, think of it as a laboratory. The atmosphere is essential. In an office, people think like office people. The environment has a profound effect on a person's thinking, either for good or bad.

2   Shape your environment so it propels you towards your ideal future. Your workplace should fit in with and encourage you to achieve your vision.

3   Make sure your workplace is an enriching and exciting place to be. It should pump energy into your work, not deaden it. Workplace restrictions prevent you from thinking freely, so work where the focus is on releasing your potential rather than keeping to rules – somewhere where you get fired for playing safe and promoted for taking risks.

Don't master your craft, be an apprentice forever

One of my students was a hugely talented fashion student. Her dream was to work for and learn from the great Alexander McQueen, the most respected name in fashion and at the peak of his career in 2005. Because he was an alumnus of Central Saint Martins, I was able to pull a few strings, and she became one of his apprentices. While he fitted clothes to a model, she was with him while cutting cloth, designing, and much more.

The apprenticeship was a disappointment. McQueen chain-smoked while working, with her handing him a new, lit cigarette the moment he finished his old one. He worked so frantically, waiting for a cigarette meant a break in his concentration. He put his hand out without looking up and expected to find a new cigarette between his fingers. She felt she wasn't learning anything, but I explained her attitude was the real problem. She was doing her job – handing him lit cigarettes – but needed to do more. It was the perfect learning opportunity. She could watch him closely, observe how he dealt with clients, other apprentices, how he worked – and, most importantly, how he thought. She started asking McQueen questions, and things opened up. He could see her genuine interest in learning. Like many great leaders, he was very open and explained his techniques. The concept was vital for him: the material he used, the design, the accessories, all hung on the idea. He had a tremendous amount of empathy with the wearer, how the clothes would make them feel as they moved, and the empowering effect on the woman wearing them. Eventually, my student was given more and more responsibility and worked her way up. Wherever you are, the person above, near or beneath you is doing something that could teach you invaluable lessons.

Anthony Caro was an apprentice of sculptor Henry Moore. At first, he performed menial chores but worked his way up to help make Moore's iconic sculptures, learning from one of the most internationally celebrated sculptors of the post-war period. Moore sketched trees and sheep and collected unusual stones, animal bones and branches on his walks in the countryside because nature inspired him. He used these irregular, contorted natural forms as inspiration for his sculptures of the human figure.

Caro left Moore's studio and became a famous artist in his own right. His work seemed to be the exact opposite of Moore's, using industrial materials like girders, whereas Moore used natural materials like stone, clay or plaster. Caro didn't base his work on the human figure. Unlike Moore, instead of the plinth, he placed his sculptures directly on the floor. Superficially it looked as if Caro had learned nothing from Moore, but although when we're young, we need a mentor, at some point we all make our own way. What Caro learned from Moore was to be true to himself and his interests. He also learned technical things like how to run a studio, handle assistants and accounts. 'Poor is the pupil who does not surpass his master,' said Leonardo da Vinci. Learning skills is not as crucial as absorbing attitudes and methods.

A leader needs an apprentice as much as an apprentice needs a leader. You learn more about what you do when you try to teach it, because when you explain how to do something, it deepens your understanding. James Cash Penney founded a shop in the US in 1901. When his wife became pregnant, he hired an assistant and taught him everything he needed to know about running the shop. When his wife wanted to return to work, he didn't want to sack his assistant, so he opened another shop and split the profits fifty-fifty with the assistant. It worked. He repeated the process, and by the 60s ended up with 1,700 stores, the biggest chain in the US. He didn't set out with a plan to become that huge. His wife became pregnant, he was decent to his staff and wanted to avoid sacking him, and it set off a chain reaction. As businessman Tom Peters said, 'Leaders don't create followers, they create more leaders.' He tried to help and teach his apprentices as much as possible, so they could become independent and think for themselves.

Many of my graphic design students come straight from school to university. At university, they study the philosophy of communication, the theory of advertising, the principles of semiotics, and much more. The intellectual approach has its place, but it can obscure the vulgar fact that they ultimately have to sell something. So I set them a task: they have to buy ten of the same product from the pound shop – sponges, washing-up liquid or any household cleaning item – then sell them door to door for £2 each. They hate it. They think it is crude and beneath them. But I set them the task to remind them of the harsh reality: they have to look someone in the eye and give them a reason to buy their sponges. I was inspired to set the project by David Ogilvy, the 'Father of Advertising'. One of his most famous straplines was, 'At 60 miles an hour the loudest noise in this new Rolls-Royce comes from the electric clock'. He started as a door-to-door salesman selling AGA ovens, and he was so good that his employer asked him to write an instruction manual to help the other salesmen. When he had the most successful advertising agency in the world and was sitting in a large leather chair in a large office, he didn't lose sight of the fact that he was still selling something like a door-to-door salesman. He thought his advertising campaigns' successes were due to a thorough understanding of the consumer and how they felt.

1 Listen. Useful information may not appear evident at first, so put aside your preconceived ideas about what is essential information. Caro learned a lot about the business side of art from Moore. Reflect on the information and think about how to use it.

2 You're always an apprentice. You're never the finished article, and there's always a new skill to learn. You might want everyone to believe you've got all the answers, but you'll fool yourself and them. Real success comes from always thinking of yourself as a student of your craft. Assuming you have all the answers will prevent you from hunting for more new ideas.

3 Ask questions. Asking questions reminds you others have worthwhile ideas. Too many leaders think their job is to dish out orders. It isn't. It is to find things out, and asking questions is the way to do that. The best leaders, like Moore, are simultaneously leaders and apprentices. Hemingway said in *The Wild Years*, 'We are all apprentices in a craft where no one ever becomes a master.'

Do the wrong thing in the right place

We often feel under pressure to produce appealing work. We want the approval of others in our field. But this leads to pleasing work, and 'pleasing' is not 'brilliant'. It seems logical to reproduce what has been popular before – but your work ends up looking the same as everyone else's. Do the wrong thing in the right place.

In the 1960s, car designers kept to the rules of the industry. They did the right thing in the right place. The result? All cars rolled off the assembly line looking like identical tin boxes.

The Jaguar car company employed aircraft designer Malcolm Sayer, who designed a car like a jet fighter plane. Uniquely, he tested prototypes in wind tunnels as he'd done with aeroplanes, and aerodynamic principles made his designs sleek and futuristic. The standard practice was to divide a car into equal thirds bonnet, body and boot, but half of Sayer's design was the bonnet, the other half the body. Sayer exhibited his E-Type Jaguar at the 1961 Geneva Motor Show and crowds flocked to see the instant classic. Enzo Ferrari called it 'the most beautiful car ever made'. It went into the Museum of Modern Art's permanent collection alongside Picassos and Monets. Sayer changed car design forever by ignoring the field's traditions. His aircraft designs were good, but they weren't brilliant. He was doing the right thing in the right place. Applying aircraft design principles to a car made his designs unique – doing the wrong thing in the right place. He didn't adapt to the industry; he dared to make the sector change to his way of designing.

We need to use all our skills, even if they come from a different field. Like Sayer, we need to use whatever attributes, resources and knowledge we have to open our minds to all we have to offer.

Imagine you're a good physicist, biologist, chemist or astrophysicist, but you want to take that extra step up to the Nobel Prize level. What would you do? Take up abstract painting? Researchers at Michigan State University studied the lives of every Nobel Prize-winning scientist from 1901 to 2005 and compared them to other successful scientists of the same period. The difference? Nobel Prize winners had a deep interest in the arts. Those with an interest in composing or playing music were twice as likely to win a Nobel Prize; an interest in painting or sculpture, seven times more likely; woodworking or glass-blowing, over seven times; writing poetry or novels, twelve times more likely; acting or dancing, twenty-two times. Creative activities outside science boost scientific imagination. Researchers call it 'integrated activity sets'. Success as a scientist is directly related to an interest in the arts because it nurtures the parts of the brain needed for innovation; the Nobel Prize winners transferred the knowledge and skills from one area to another. It also works the other way around: artists with an interest in the sciences transfer those ideas and enrich their work.

Part of my job has been to look through the portfolios of prospective students at art colleges. Being accepted or rejected could change their lives, but truthfully, most folios are predictable. I've seen 99 per cent of the work before because they've all read the same books, and visited similar galleries. They're not precisely the same, of course, but the same sort of stuff. Once a student came in who had left school at sixteen and gone to work in an aircraft factory riveting the aluminium fuselages and wings together. He was apologetic for his lack of formal education, but he produced sculptures of strange aerodynamic shapes made of riveted aluminium and we'd never seen anything like it. We were riveted (no joke). It was the most exciting portfolio we'd seen for years. He designed and made sculptures like an aircraft designer – like Sayer – and his work was startling and different because his influences were not from the art world. We're often so immersed in our field, we forget to use the skills we've learned elsewhere. The expertise we get from our domain is the same everyone else is using. Throw in a passion from another area of your life.

1 Be aware you have unconsciously absorbed the influences of your field. Seek influences from outside to give you new perspectives.

2 Transfer ideas from an interest in music, sport, literature or anywhere, to your sphere. As a creative consultant for diverse organizations and industries, I have

little knowledge of banks, hospitals or
computer manufacturers, so I give
them fresh new insights from a
different perspective.

I was asked by
MasterCard to devise online
creative thinking exercises for
employees of banks throughout
the world, no matter how elevated or
lowly their position. I knew I could help them
introduce fresh ideas to their roles.

3   If you adopt the accepted standards, your work becomes
standard. If you've been doing the right thing in the right place,
try doing the wrong thing in the right place – new possibilities
will open up. Get the correct result
by doing the wrong thing.

Three ways you'll benefit from transparency

You have a great idea, a bestseller and a blockbuster. Your instinct is to covet it and hide it, so it's not stolen. But a concept is a seed that needs to grow, and a seed can't grow in a desert; it needs water and nutrients. Why not share it and let other people help you?

One of the most disruptive forces to emerge from social media is transparency. Individuals and small companies are more open to sharing their ideas and processes than big organizations. Their audience becomes engaged, and in turn, spreads the word. Show what you do, and others will become interested because you establish authenticity, trust and credibility.

In the early 80s, I walked into a furniture shop called One Off in London's Covent Garden, in a crumbling building with bare brick walls and a concrete floor. It was an upmarket shop, and the furniture was skilfully displayed, but it was also a laboratory and workshop where you could see them designing and making the furniture. One Off was a cross between a steel foundry and an art gallery. The brainchild of designer Ron Arad, anyone could walk in and watch him welding and cutting metal, and talk either to him or to his assistants and even make suggestions. As the playwright George Bernard Shaw said, 'If you have an apple and I have an apple, and we exchange these apples, then you and I will still each have one apple. But if you have an idea and I have an idea, and we exchange these ideas, then each of us will have two ideas.' The place emanated a spirit of generosity, and Arad put new ideas out there for everyone to see. Drawings of fresh designs covered the walls. It was a brilliant public showcase and attracted the press and public in droves. Arad was talked about, written about, and built up followers by being transparent. He didn't need to spend money on advertising because of his openness; he was splashed all over the media. It was fascinating. I watched them making a Rover Chair, a fusion of a red leather car seat from a scrapped Rover car, and a bent scaffolding frame. I felt compelled to buy it for £99, although that was a lot in 1981. Those pieces of furniture are now worth thousands of dollars each and are in every major museum.

Recently, I walked into an exhibition of Louis Vuitton's work in the Strand in London. I'd always thought it was ridiculous to pay thousands for a Louis Vuitton handbag – it's just a handbag. I assumed people were buying the brand name and the status. But the exhibition gave you an insight into the creative processes of Louis Vuitton. It showed hundreds of sketches and prototypes; a craftsman had flown over from Italy with his entire workshop. It took you through the process of making a handbag and projected the details onto mirrored walls, pure white figurative sculptures and massive digital screens. They designed the exhibition for photo opportunities and to share; they were proud of the dedication they put into their work and wanted everyone to see. The exhibition dominated everyone's Instagram feed for weeks. There were free posters and stickers to take away. I added up all the working hours and resources that went into a handbag and wondered how they could sell them for so little.

If you hide your process, people never fully understand your work or the effort that went into it. Let people see into your mind and workshop. Let them see how your ideas develop, and people will be able to relate to you and your work. If your audience understands how you created your work, they are more likely to buy into it.

1   Show everyone the nuts and bolts of your project. Reveal how it developed step by step. Don't sweep mistakes under the rug but show them and how you overcame them.

2   Transparency helps you build a better relationship with your audience because they understand you better. When you're transparent, you show you've nothing to hide and establish yourself as credible – so people trust you.

3   Transparency is an essential element of leadership. Ron Arad became a leader in his field and leader of a large company of assistants by gaining their trust with openness.

I shared the process of writing and illustrating this book online. Take a look on my Instagram account, @rod.judkins.

Be an expander, not a restrictor

Those who are ten times as successful as you aren't ten times as talented – they're thinking ten times bigger. Many people trap themselves in the small time with their small-scale thinking. The abilities needed to make a small task successful are virtually the same as those required to make a large project successful. Decide to scale up and expand your idea. If you can design a kettle, you can design a chair, if a chair, then a car, a car, then a building, and a building a town. The same principle is true in every sphere of life. Think ten times bigger and think ten times better.

When you have an idea, assess if it can be scaled up. Many small ideas have the potential for almost limitless growth. If it can't be scaled up, discard it.

Architects have a saying: 'from the spoon to the city'. It's a way to remind them that something small, like a spoon, is as essential as a building. It takes as long to design a spoon as it does a building because the process is the same. If your spoon cuts your mouth, spills your custard or is hard to hold, it ruins your day as much as a poorly designed building. The spoon is something you directly interact with and can make your day great or bad. Great designers like Philippe Starck began their careers creating small objects like toothbrushes and kettles. They magnify the same principles to more significant objects like bicycles, cars, ships and buildings. Use small objects to explore ideas on a manageable scale, but then expand them.

Some houses and offices contain so many of his chairs, tables, lemon squeezers and kitchen utensils it's as if they are a Philippe Starck museum. Anita Roddick said she learned everything about running multimillion-pound business The Body Shop from first running a small seaside café. If you can direct a thirty-second ad, you can make a feature-length film (Ridley Scott, David Fincher and Guillermo del Toro all started as directors of television commercials). TV ads taught them how to tell a story in a pared-down, engaging, visually appealing way. They learned how to interpret a screenplay, how to direct actors, how to run a film crew (commercials have huge camera crews like a movie) and become master storytellers.

I'll leave you to define what success is for you; it could be to start your own business or to raise money for charity. But take your definition and raise the bar. The scale of

your thinking dictates the size of your achievements, so think of yourself as a magnifier, not a reducer. A magnifier continually searches for ways to advance and elevate their work. A reducer is tight and restricts growth. Your actions either expand what you're doing and release everyone around you to help and add to your work,

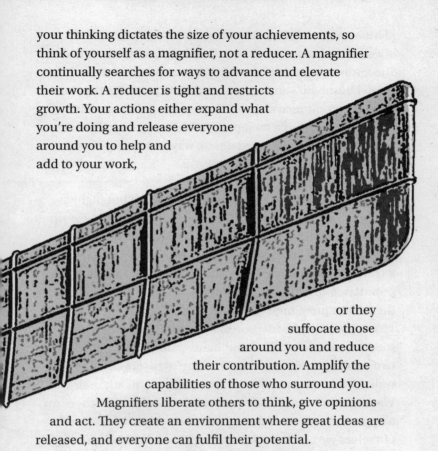

or they suffocate those around you and reduce their contribution. Amplify the capabilities of those who surround you. Magnifiers liberate others to think, give opinions and act. They create an environment where great ideas are released, and everyone can fulfil their potential.

Artist Antony Gormley made small sculptures of angels. Modern angels with aeroplane wings, some were only a few inches high, and others were casts of his own body in metal with wings attached. He was asked by Gateshead council to produce a sculpture near the A1 – the main road to the north of England. At first, he wasn't interested in creating 'roundabout art', but when he walked up the huge hill and saw its proposed position, he realized the potential. Gormley was surprised when a local councillor suggested it needed one of his angels, scaled up. The result, the Angel of the North, is a steel sculpture 20 metres tall with wings 54 metres wide. The impressive scale is shocking. It proves American architect Daniel Burnham's advice, 'make no little plans, for they have no magic to stir men's blood'. The local population came to love the statue as a metaphor for their robust and resilient culture. Gormley has an expansive way of thinking about his work.

Artist Ai Wei Wei was fascinated by the small but highly symbolic sunflower seeds. They were a typical Chinese street snack and reminded him of when he'd had little money and shared the seeds with friends. When Ai Wei Wei was a child, posters showed Chairman Mao as the sun and the population of China as sunflowers. In 2010, Wei Wei filled the 3,500 square metres of Tate Modern's Turbine Hall with 100 million handmade porcelain sunflower seeds. Each seed was moulded, fired and hand-painted in China over two years by 1,600 artisans. The Tate's visitors could touch, walk on and listen to the seeds rattle underneath their feet. We can either see our ideas on a small scale or see them on a large scale – it's a matter of our perception. We can tell ourselves we are a small player or a significant player. Big thinking stimulates the optimism to undertake significant projects; working out how to do them develops from believing they're possible. Big thinking leads to substantial actions. It's not about intelligence, because the clever are equally susceptible to talking themselves down and generating self-doubt. It's your thinking that holds you back. You need to be aware of any tendency to think small and safe, and counteract it.

To give your work impact, experiment with the scale. Extreme scale gives work impact and makes it memorable; Georgia O'Keeffe said she painted a flower on an enormous scale, so 'you could not ignore its beauty'. Her crucial asset was her perception of herself as an artist who could produce large-scale works as big and as confident as those of the male artists working at the time. The art world had a limited view of what a woman could achieve, but O'Keeffe had an 'expander' mindset. When Francis Ford Coppola proudly presented the initial cut of *The Godfather* to producer Robert Evans, Evans said it looked like 'a long bad trailer for a really good film' and asked him to add an hour to give it more gravitas and an epic feel. It became one of the highest-grossing films in history. Coppola was lucky Evans was a natural expander.

1   Whatever level you are at, step up to the next. Don't start anything without the potential for expansion. Average scale equals average impact. Disregard where you are, and aim at what you want to become. Think big from the start.

2   Maintain a consistently high quality. Don't let quality deteriorate if your business or work expands, but maintain quality throughout. It's no use producing something big but weak and inferior.

3   Take it one decision and deal with one problem at a time. Scaling up creates problems, so you should deal with them step by step or they become overwhelming.

Overcome resistance

We have all come up against resistance to our ideas. The creative want to experiment and break new ground, but opposition to new ideas often surrounds us. When a technician or administrator says, 'It can't be done,' what they mean is, it's too much trouble for them. Society and organizations like to stick with what they know; they resist and put obstacles in the way of innovation. Anyone trying to get a project underway comes up against people who say, 'It's too costly' or 'It's already been done' or 'It's too much trouble.'

We have to overcome the inertia of others and the barriers they set up. See it as part of the excitement of being creative and what makes you different. To keep to your vision and prove everyone wrong, you'll have to do things for yourself. The cost might be high in money and time, but in the end it's all the more rewarding.

The famous husband and wife design team Charles and Ray Eames were determined to produce visionary, futuristic furniture. They were desperate to explore the possibilities of furniture design and make bold unique shapes. In the 1940s, they had the idea of using bent plywood as a material. They asked manufacturers to invest in developing a machine to do this but all the companies refused, citing their technicians' reasons why it was impossible: 'too expensive,' 'too time-consuming,' 'not practically possible.'

Charles and Ray were furniture makers, not engineers, but they spent months in their kitchen developing a machine from pieces of a bicycle, plaster moulds and parts of electric fires. It enabled them to press, heat and glue thin plywood layers together, and created extraordinary furniture. Their dynamic, modern work was a massive success with the public, and when they could *see* the benefits, manufacturers made the machines. Bent plywood quickly became the most fashionable furniture designer's material.

Finding a way around restrictions is what makes creative people unique. Imagine if there were no limitations, no one saying, 'It can't be done'. There would be no need for you to show your ingenuity or creativity.

An ad agency was struggling with an idea for a TV ad. The problem was that the client had put ten mandatories on the brief: no comedy, must include a product demo, a particular setting, blah, blah, blah . . . The cost of advertising scares the client, so they lay down restrictions to keep control. But a good brief shouldn't include any mandatories – limitations impede an agency's thinking. A TV ad was a great showcase for the agency to do creative work and, frustrated by the limits, they asked me to join as a consultant. They were disappointed when I said they'd have to make the uncreative ad the client wanted, but I suggested, 'Let's make two ads: the limited one the client wants and the unlimited one we want.'

Firstly, they made the ad with the client's mandatories. It was good, but it wasn't brilliant. Secondly, we filmed the agency's inventive film with no restrictions, tapping freely into their creativity and making the ad they most wanted to see. Although it was filmed on a shoestring budget, using friends, relatives, acquaintances and anyone to act or help out, it was entertaining and brilliant.

We showed the client both ads, and they chose to air both. The creative one was the most popular with the public. In the end, the client and the agency both got what they wanted. Work out what restrictions are holding you back and don't let the negativity and inertia of others affect you. Getting around them is part of being creative.

1 When people tell you 'it can't be done', it's down to you to show them it can. Brilliant work crashes into new areas and that makes it worrying for organizations. You'll have to convince them by showing them it's possible. When someone tells you 'it can't be done', they're telling you their limitations, not yours. Let them think you 'can't do it' if they want. But go ahead and prove you can. The successful do the difficult things the unsuccessful avoid.

2 See obstacles as an opportunity to exercise creative thinking. In the 1960s, Hungary wasn't a good country in which to be an artist. Censors for the authoritarian, repressive regime analysed even the most subtle artwork for hidden meaning. For artist Károly Kismányoky, it was the perfect culture for conceptual art. He produced a visually striking, iconic work: photographs of his own face with cut-outs of other people's eyes covering his. It was a comment on a country of surveillance. Circumventing tyranny forced him to think of brilliant ideas. Whatever obstacles are blocking your path, finding a way around them could lead you to original and surprising solutions.

Set your sights too high

Most people set themselves sensible, achievable goals. That's why they only ever attain sensible, achievable goals. Set out to do what you know you're capable of, and it's all you'll accomplish. 'The greater danger for most of us lies not in setting our aim too high and falling short, but in setting our aim too low, and achieving our mark,' said Michelangelo.

'Ambition makes you look pretty ugly,' sang Radiohead. The lyrics are from the song 'Paranoid Android', and refer to materialists who seek wealth at all costs. Radiohead had high aspirations for the song and spent a lot of time recording, rerecording and editing. Ambition drives you to pour time and effort into your work and overcome obstacles, but it must be consciously directed to worthwhile work, not shallow goals.

A friend of mine was a student on an art foundation course at Leeds Arts University. A male student stood out to her and the others as the least likely to succeed: he had a grade E in Art A level, washed pots in a restaurant, did poorly on the course, and worked on building sites afterwards. He applied for a Fine Arts degree course at Goldsmiths University, and was rejected twice.

What surprised others was that he dared to see Pablo Picasso as his benchmark. He said, 'What I like about Picasso are all the money things, the fame, the stardom, the signing of the cheques and people not cashing them because they've got his signature on.' Picasso would write a cheque for a meal, and the restaurateur wouldn't cash it because the signature was more valuable. Signing a restaurant bill was a sign that an artist was recognized in the same way as a film or football star, and Picasso's significance was that he wasn't just respected in the narrow confines of the art scene but famous in the world. His ambition meant that he reached out beyond the art establishment to ordinary members of the public – including restaurant owners.

Goldsmiths eventually accepted the student, who had produced more inventive work in the meantime: that student was Damien Hirst. At Goldsmiths, something clicked, which led him to become one of the most significant artists of his generation. Hirst had many brilliant ideas, but his vision of who he could be was his most impressive. His own signature is now worth over £300. He said, 'If I sign a cheque in a restaurant and it's for £150, the cheque is actually worth more than the bill comes to.' Money is a good way to measure your work, but it doesn't calculate value because value is based on the wider contribution to culture. Hirst was ambitious, not just for his work, but for art. At that time, the art world looked inwards and spoke to itself, not the wider public. Hirst shows how worthwhile ambition can transform you from an underachiever to an overachiever.

The research of Timothy Judge and John Kammeyer-Mueller of the University of Florida established that 'ambition has stronger effects on career and life success' than inherited personality traits, 'ability, and socioeconomic status'. They proved ambition was more important for educational attainment, higher wages, promotion, success and greater life satisfaction.

Picasso spoke to a broader public than just the art world, and Hirst followed his example. Hirst's retrospectives at major museums drew record-breaking crowds. His early work, such as *A Thousand Years* from 1990, is remarkable because he wanted to speak not just to the art elite, but to the person on the street in the same way as films, music and novels do. Hirst described *A Thousand Years* as a 'life cycle in a box'. It was a huge, twelve-feet-long, rectangular glass case with a severed cow's head lying at the bottom and an insect-electrocuting light suspended above it. Maggots ate the cow's head, metamorphosed into flies and struck the fly-killer. The dead flies accumulated into a pile. Hirst forced the viewer to face life and death. He explained, 'You can frighten people with death or an idea of their own mortality, or it can actually give them vigour.' It was written about in art magazines, but also widely reported in newspapers and television that had previously mocked modern art but now took it seriously. Most people are comfortable talking to others in their sphere, to preach to the converted, because communicating directly to the public is more difficult.

1　　Don't be afraid to have an unreasonable goal: to run a Michelin-starred restaurant, rid the seas of plastic, have a one-person exhibition at the Tate Gallery, or write a million-copy-selling book. Set your sights unrealistically high and you might look ridiculous to others, but that doesn't matter. We often suppress big ambitions because our friends tell us we're unrealistic.

Eventually, they become internal voices: 'I'm not smart enough' or 'I haven't got the financial backing'. Ninety-nine per cent of people believe they can't achieve great things, so they set realistic goals; but 'realistic' goals are more competitive and harder to achieve. Hirst was floundering before he found his ambition. He had little skill as a painter or sculptor; his outstanding gift was ambition. Ambition can be cultivated and managed by individuals and organizations to achieve brilliant advances in science, business or art. The poverty of people's aspirations is a tragedy of their own making.

2   Attune your greatest ambition with a clear route to your goal; it will fuel your energy and drive to achieve it. If you can pair your dream with a love of your subject and achieving worthwhile goals, you'll have a winning combination.

Create friction

A young, unknown rock musician asked his friend an inspired question: 'How successful do you think a band could be if they mixed heavy Black Sabbath with the Beatles?' The answer was – the most famous on the planet. Creative ideas often start by setting up an unlikely contrast and watching the sparks and energy fly out as they rub together.

The rock musician raised the question because, as he put it, 'I didn't think we were really original enough'. The mixture was put together in an album called *Nevermind*, the band was Nirvana, and the musician was – of course – Kurt Cobain. The heavy metal, thrashing guitars pumping out melodic, beautifully structured tunes was a completely new sound and Nirvana became the most influential band of the 90s. *Nevermind* has since sold over 10 million copies. At first, Nirvana was just another unexceptional band; their early recordings lack originality. But Cobain was searching for a way to make them unique, and contrast was his solution. It worked. Does your project have two contrasting elements crashing into each other? Like Cobain, we should be striving to create friction and energy.

The great composer Gustav Mahler arranged a consultation session with psychiatrist Sigmund Freud. Creative people always reach a point in their career when they want to gain a deeper understanding of their motivation and drive, and Freud was able to uncover the secret of Mahler's success.

In a four-hour psychoanalytic session, Freud coaxed Mahler into recalling an incident that had left an indelible impression on his subconscious. When Mahler was a child, his household was turbulent and emotional. His parents were under tremendous pressure because they had fourteen children, and Mahler's father ran a tavern and distillery. One day his parents had a furious argument, and Mahler ran out of the house. A barrel organ was playing a light-hearted, chirpy tune in the street. Freud noted that 'the conjunction of high tragedy and light amusement was from then on inextricably fixed in his mind'. The happy/sad contrast was the key to Mahler's success. Once he was aware of the connection, he exaggerated and exploited it in more depth.

Picture an early morning in one of California's wealthiest neighbourhoods. The camera pans slowly across a vast, majestic mansion situated in an idyllic, quiet, perfectly manicured garden. The camera lingers inside the comfortable, luxurious house and gradually moves into an expensively decorated bedroom. Hollywood mogul Jack Woltz is asleep in a massive bed with silk sheets. Leisurely, he awakes. He senses something isn't right. Then he screams in terror, because the severed head of his prize racehorse lies next to him. Blood covers his bed . . . This gruesome scene is from the film *The Godfather*, and the shock comes from the long, slow build-up. The film varies its rhythm throughout, lulling you with long quiet episodes at a slow, brooding pace, punctuated by fast-paced, loud, violent scenes.

Striking oppositions within your work create impact and drama, and power friction and energy. A tragic event in a novel has more effect if it follows a comic scene. If everything is funny, nothing is funny. If everything is sad, nothing is sad.

But funny, sad, funny, sad keeps your audience on edge and leaves an impression. This switch from fast to slow, hard to soft engages the audience because they don't know what's coming next.

The Royal Ontario Museum was originally housed entirely in an austere, ancient fortress. The unwelcoming and defensive exterior worked for a fort, but a museum should draw people inside. The unforgettable Michael Lee-Chin Crystal was a striking addition to the original building. Designed by architect Daniel Libeskind, the Crystal was the opposite of the original building – an open, welcoming modern space blurring the distinction between the street and the interior. The contrast is striking. Modern/ancient; light/dark; friendly/ unfriendly; glass/stone; flat/jagged. The inspiring atmosphere of a dynamic centre of learning transformed the museum into a world-class destination and inspired a renewed interest.

No one uses the device of contrasts more effectively than Charles Dickens. In *A Tale of Two Cities*, he opens with, 'It was the best of times, it was the worst of times, it was the age of wisdom, it was the age of foolishness, it was the epoch of belief, it was the epoch of incredulity, it was the season of Light, it was the season of Darkness, it was the spring of hope, it was the winter of despair . . .'

Dickens hits us right from the start with contrasts, and these contrasts constantly reappear during the novel and influence the characters' lives. Dickens used them to help explain ideas because it made his argument stronger and more memorable, as well as surprising the audience and adding drama. Contrast helps to highlight the attributes of each element; for example, a generous character appears more generous next to a miserly character, and vice versa. A blue swimming pool looks bluer with an orange inflatable floating on it. Pianist Janine Parsons explained, 'A common problem for beginners is their fear of bold contrast. The decision to reduce the tonal range in this way is a misguided attempt to draw attention away from any errors. It only robs the work of vitality and depth.'

1   Think of opposites you can put together; the more unlikely, the better. The challenge is in putting them together in a way that creates friction but also makes them work together. *The Simpsons* creator Matt Groening contrasts Homer with Lisa: stupid/smart, fat/skinny, male/female, middle-aged/young, lazy/energetic, wears blue/wears red, and so on. Homer has more impact next to his opposite character. There is also more room to create misunderstandings and clashes between the characters.

2   Create tension. Your audience must wonder what's coming next. Great art lies in the tension between ugliness and beauty, or playfulness and severity. 'The realization that reason and anti-reason, sense and nonsense, design and chance, consciousness and unconsciousness, belong together as necessary parts of a whole – this was the central message of Dada,' said artist Hans Richter. Put the extraordinary next to the extraordinary, and they both look ordinary. The same thinking applies to any medium.

Think outwards, not inwards

Sometimes we get so entranced with our work that we forget about the audience. We are so in love with what we're doing, we forget to ask if anyone else will be.

It's surprising how great artists, designers and business leaders are not self-obsessed but 'peoplecentric'. They know that if they have a deep understanding of their audience, they'll know what will have a big impact on them. Focus on thinking outwards and not inwards – it's easy to get so wrapped up in your own concerns that you forget your work has to communicate to others.

I visited the crowded Café Costes in Paris in the 1980s. The customers were drawn by its reputation for great design and the chance to sit on a three-legged chair designed specifically for the café by Philippe Starck, who had previously spent hours in the café and noticed that waiters kept tripping over rear chair legs. With only one rear leg, they tripped less often. The French waiters were still rude but at least they spilt less coffee over you. The small improvement had big consequences for Starck: Café Costes soon closed but crowds flocked to buy the chair. It became iconic, and it's still an international bestseller. Starck didn't dream up an interesting shape for the sake of it; the design grew out of consideration for the waiters.

Starck also used humour to transform the normally dull task of using the men's room in the Peninsula Hotel in Hong Kong. Men pee onto the city – or at least that's how it feels. They pee on a glass window overlooking the city. A complex system of sensors and water jets cleans it all away.

Be 'peoplecentric'. Analyse how others behave. If you're designing software, watch people use it and notice when they grimace – then fix it. Artist Max Ernst's paintings help everyone appreciate the importance of the subconscious by visualizing it to show the strange workings of our minds. Jean-Paul Sartre emphasized the control we have over ourselves and made us aware we should learn to take responsibility for our own decisions and actions.

An electric toothbrush company consulted me about a new product they were developing. The toothbrush bombarded users with information about which areas they hadn't cleaned, their gum health and much more. The technicians loved adding features. I asked my young, tech-savvy art students to try out the prototypes. They hated it because it made them worry about this and worry about that; they were fed up with technology telling them what they should and shouldn't do. The techies had got carried away with what they could add, and had forgotten that their job was to make cleaning your teeth enjoyable. So we scrapped all the new features except two: automatically ordering replacement heads via a Bluetooth app, and telling you when the toothbrush needed charging. When it was released, it outsold the more technical competitors. Adding features is a good idea, but don't get carried away and throw things in unless they are actually helpful.

Myspace and Facebook had the same idea at roughly the same time. Myspace was the social media leader when it launched, but didn't consider its users as well as Facebook did. Myspace were more interested in advertising (in other words, making themselves money), while Facebook was interested in their site being easy, fun and entertaining. Everyone switched to them.

1   Your work is not a soliloquy, it's a conversation. When I walk around Tate Modern, the Guggenheim or the New York Met, and look at the work of Mark Rothko, Barbara Kruger, Bruce Nauman, Louise Bourgeois and others, I find myself in conversation with the artwork. It's not a one-way street. The artists have thought about how an audience will react to their work.

2   Get a deep insight into your field. Many young artists work for a gallery when they're young – they want to find out how the whole system works. Keith Haring worked as a gallery assistant for the Tony Shafrazi Gallery, where he later had his breakthrough exhibition. Shafrazi said that Keith was incredibly intelligent, working while listening and paying attention and fine tuning himself all the time.

Be exceptionally average

If you target the average your work will be average. We often want our work to appeal to as many people as possible, so we build things around an idea of the average person. Don't aim to please the average person. They don't exist.

When Jewish families fled the Nazis they could only take essentials, usually whatever they could fit in a suitcase. When Sigmund Freud fled the Nazis he also took what was essential – his chair. As his daughter Mathilde observed, he was most at ease in an unusual sitting position, 'with his legs draped over one arm of his chair, his book held high and his neck unsupported', so he commissioned craftsmen to create a unique, custom-made chair design with armrests doubling as backrests. The chair still looks ultramodern. It mirrored his thinking that we are all unique and one size does not fit all. Before Freud, a standardized treatment was given to all

patients, but he tailored his treatment to the individual. He looked at their history, circumstances and personality. In the same way, he didn't try to fit into an average chair, he made an individual chair to fit his individual needs. In formulating treatment to fit the individual, Freud created modern psychoanalysis. He didn't worry much about what others thought of him; his ideas about sex and the subconscious outraged the public but eventually their true worth and usefulness won through. His chair also struck a chord with and influenced designers. Conventional chair designers use a diagram of the average specifications of the human figure – which is why bus, train and aircraft seats are so uncomfortable. Don't try to please the average person because they don't exist.

One of my favourite book titles is Sigmund Freud's *The Psychopathology of Everyday Life*. At the time Freud wrote it, the mentally ill were reviled as 'other'; they failed to fit into society's idea of 'normal.' But Freud discovered that the mechanisms of mental illness are in all of us; they're 'everyday'. Freud's conclusion was to see the mentally ill as 'everyday' and treat them with compassion, because we all have the tendency within us.

When I work with companies who talk about their average customer, I get them to investigate and question some of their 'average' customers. Then they discover that they're anything but average . . .

1 Don't make average people, experiences and products the targets of your work. If you do, your work will appeal to fewer people, not more.

2 If you feel like you don't fit in, it's because you don't; but if you don't fit in, it doesn't mean there's something wrong with you. Don't change yourself or force yourself to conform. Make things that fit in with you. What makes you different is the pearl in the oyster – take it out and show it off. You are here to make a difference, and you can't make a difference unless you are different. You're not here to fit in. You're here to stick out.

Grow your strength from your weakness

We ignore a weakness and hope we'll sort it out later. But don't avoid the fault in your project or yourself, confront it from the start. If you attack it in the right way, you could turn it into strength.

In humid tropical conditions, the weakest point of wooden furniture was joints. Damp made them unstable and shaky, but chair designers continued to use them because it was standard practice. The designer Gerald Summers worked in Singapore and attacked this weakness with his first commission. He cut four straight lines in a single sheet of wood, then pressed it in a mould to create the curve of the chair's legs and arms. His Bent Plywood Armchair of 1934 had no joints. And there was a bonus – it was original and distinctive.

Tackle a weakness at the outset; make it the strength. It could be the key to unlocking brilliance. Novelist James Joyce was weak at writing gripping plots, so he made a feature of producing novels with no narrative. Andy Warhol's weakness was a poor sense of colour. His work is instantly recognizable for deliberately vulgar, clashing colours. Look for the weakest link in your project. Start there.

Upton Sinclair decided to run for governor of California. But he was a writer and had no political experience. Back in the 1930s, the public voted for candidates with political experience; a pilot got a job if he had flown hundreds of hours, a CEO if he had already run a company. The situation seemed hopeless. Sinclair used his inexperience as the basis for his campaign, and his tactics made history. He was hardly registering in the polls until he addressed his weakness, but when he did, the electorate found him refreshing. 'One of the most dramatic and influential contests in California history, it helped change the political landscape of the nation,' wrote the University of Washington's blog.

Falling apart at the seams

Sinclair wrote a pamphlet entitled *I, Governor of California and How I Ended Poverty: A True Story of the Future*. In it he envisaged his nomination, victory and successful implementation of his EPIC programme, 'End Poverty in California'. His book described far-reaching transformations such as abolishing the sales tax, a universal pension plan, and repurposing discarded land and factories to help the unemployed return to work. He used his abilities as a writer to touch people in a way no politician could, and everyone could picture the result of his policies. Suddenly the standard strategies of politicians worked against them.

The book was an immediate bestseller. Thousands rallied around its message, and it became a mass political movement. Sinclair blew away the Democratic opposition to capture the primary. His success continued into the general election campaign. From nowhere, he jumped to the lead. Because he was a writer and not a politician, he brought new, creative ideas and methods to the campaign, and the opposition was forced to be innovative and poured millions into the first-ever TV and cinema negative ads. Many credit him for changing

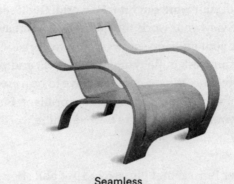

Seamless

political tactics. In the end, he narrowly lost, but his strategy and the 'attack ads' launched against him still reverberate through modern politics.

Don't turn a blind eye to your weakness; give it your full attention. The problem is your assumptions about what is a strength or a weakness, and your weakness is often your weakness because you think of it that way. 'Our strength grows out of our weaknesses,' said Ralph Waldo Emerson. Work out how to turn your weakness into power.

Follow Picasso's advice on how to build a creative career

The problem for any young person, start-up, or someone beginning a new career is, how do you earn a living from doing what you love?

The most crucial step for any creative person is – build a following! Get your work out into the world. Get it seen. The more people view your work, the quicker you'll create an audience. As your audience grows, your prices rise. Overprice yourself or your work initially and it won't sell, and you'll have nothing to build on. What fuels your drive to be a creator and a maker is your ego, producing something brilliant. But if you're not careful, your ego can start to believe you're worth more than you are.

Photographer Brassaï met Picasso in 1944 and showed him drawings he'd done many years before. Picasso was infuriated that Brassaï had stopped drawing and insisted he exhibit them, saying, 'One must have the courage of one's vocation and the courage to make a living from one's vocation. The "second career" is an illusion! I was often broke too, and I always resisted any temptation to live any other way than from my painting . . . In the beginning, I did not sell at a high price, but I sold.' Picasso was exasperated at Brassaï's lack of faith in his own work. If you don't have confidence in your work, why would anyone else? But if you believe in what you do, others will be convinced. Young artists, new start-ups and organizations are always full of flaws and failings. You can't wait till everything is perfect. You have to put your work out there and see what reaction it gets. Don't have a plan B; it distracts you from plan A.

Picasso said, 'It's often been said that an artist ought to work for himself, for the "love of art", that he ought to have contempt for success. Untrue! An artist needs success.' It's always surprising how down to earth professional artists are about the commercial aspect of being an artist. It's the amateurs who have fanciful, high-minded ideas; the professional artists get on with the day-to-day slog. Picasso advised Brassaï, 'Don't price them too high. What matters is that you sell a large number of them. Your drawings must go out into the world.' It's a common mistake of young creative people that they overcharge. They need to sell their work cheaply at first – even Picasso did that for many years – then slowly build a following. Your aim should be to get your work seen by as many people as possible and don't make money your primary concern.

1   Have faith in your work. Don't have a second career. Throw all your time and effort into one job – whatever you most want to do. The struggle to earn a living in the early days adds to your sense that you're doing something worthwhile. If you don't have 100 per cent belief in what you're doing, why should anyone else?

2   Provide your services or products cheaply at first. Build up interest and a following. Selling your work raises your profile and enables you to finance yourself.

3   Picasso believed it was a myth you had to give up your integrity to make money. Integrity is about doing your very best. People will pay for excellence. You don't have to be poor to be faithful to your vocation.

Transform a scar into gold

We tend to pick up from our culture that we should aim for perfection in our relationships, work and personal life. If we strive for perfection, we automatically assume flaws should be eradicated or hidden.

The flaws in yourself or your work add character and authenticity – they are an asset in disguise. Don't cover them up. Accentuate them. Be open to the possibility that these deficiencies are the best things in your work.

Most restoration proposals for the Neues Museum in Berlin suggested flattening the ancient ruin and replacing it with a shiny new building. Architect David Chipperfield, however, proposed keeping the smashed-up old fragments but joining them together with new structures. In 1997 Chipperfield won the proposal and lovingly preserved the remains of the roofless ruin's inner walls, which were pockmarked by shell holes and the scars of war. Then he framed them with fresh, modern concrete and marble to draw visitors' attention to them.

Finding a way to incorporate flaws is beneficial because they provide charm and authenticity. We all have flaws, and it's easier to relate to someone or something equally imperfect. When the Beatles were recording their album *Abbey Road*, the Moog synthesizer developed a fault. It lost its sustain, so that if you played a note on the keyboard and took your finger off, it would glide down to the lowest note. George Harrison liked the effect and used it on 'Here Comes the Sun'. It added something unusual, unexpected and quirky.

You choose how you look at things and whether to see something as a flaw – it's just a matter of perspective. We see flaws as obstacles to overcome and put right, but if you deliberately alter your perspective, you can see them as a quality to be used. How we interpret things creates a framework for our project. If you perceive things with an open mind, a flaw can become an opportunity. You can choose to see pockmarked walls and a broken Moog synthesizer as flawed, or as a chance to produce something brilliant.

In fifteenth-century Japan, Ashikaga Yoshimasa was distraught when his precious tea bowl smashed. He sent it to be restored but was horrified by the hideous metal staples the repairers used. But the 'ugliness' was inspirational to craftsmen; they appreciated the honesty of repairing the damage so openly. The bowl became highly valued, and because the clamps looked like a locust, it was named *Bakōhan* (large-locust clamp). Japanese artisans searched for other ways to repair obviously, and collectors began to smash pots on purpose so they could fix them with gold seams, a practice that became known as *Kintsugi*. The gold highlighted the damage and added to the bowl's history and significance.

The bowls became a celebration of flaws and liberated artisans from perfectionism – there was no pressure to be faultless. The fragile ceramics became a metaphor for the human body and how everyone picks up scars and scratches. In the same way that something broken can be repaired and declare its repair, we should find positive ways to deal with traumatic events because these experiences make us unique.

We have to get into the mindset of embracing imperfection. Many artists deliberately add flaws to their work because flaws are an integral part of being human. Navajo rug weavers leave small imperfections along the borders in a line called a 'spirit line'. Japanese artisans see deliberate asymmetry, roughness, cracks and defects as essential ingredients, because nothing can maintain perfection.

Be a design hacker

We tend to accept things the way they are because it's easy. A design hacker, however, refuses to accept things the way they are and uses playful cleverness to reshape the world the way they want it, adapting the world to their needs. You too can hack into things and alter them to suit you.

Charles Darwin is famous for evolution – the evolution of the office chair. Darwin was a workaholic and needed to move around his office more easily to examine his specimens. He hacked off his static chair legs and replaced them with legs from his bed that had castors, so that the chair could move and dart around his office. He changed how people thought about office chairs, and later, designers followed his lead and office chairs evolved to be highly adjustable and moveable. I've visited his study in the Darwin Museum to see the fossilized relic of the office chair's first form. Inventing the first office chair may seem trivial compared to *On the Origin of Species*, but the instinct to be subversive, to hack into something, to question it and improve it, no matter what anyone else thought, was the same. Darwin thought of everything as malleable, whether it was an object or a theory.

Jack Smith had an idea when he was driving home, and phoned his friend Sabeer Bhatia on his mobile. After hearing one sentence, the power of the concept inspired Bhatia. It went off in his mind like an explosion, and he said, 'Oh my!

Hang up that cellular and call me back on a secure line when you get to your house! We don't want anyone to overhear!'

When they finally talked it through, their minds raced along, leaping from one suggestion to the next. Bhatia couldn't sleep and stayed up all night, scribbling down all his strategies. The next day he was afraid to speak to anyone in case he inadvertently mentioned the idea. Bhatia understood this new media was so innovative it meant you didn't need the right connections; you didn't need a track record; all you needed was an idea. He had one worth US$400 million.

But they needed finance, so they put their idea to venture capitalist Tim Draper. He loved the idea: free web-based email offered directly to the public, Hotmail. But Draper wondered how to spread it. Conventional advertising – billboards, TV and radio ads – were too costly. Then Draper had an idea that changed marketing forever. Hack into their own product. Add a message to the end of every email: 'PS. I love you. Get your free email at Hotmail.' They could advertise their product for free. A self-perpetuating marketing machine that got the message out to hundreds of thousands. The young tech company hacked into your email by adding their own ad and spread the word for free.

The belief that you can alter or change anything is a valuable mindset. Hotmail expanded faster than any media company in history.

Adopt a design hacker's mindset and don't tolerate things you're dissatisfied with – whether in business, science, or art and design. Hack into them and remake them in a way that makes more sense to you.

1   Nothing is static or finished. I once did some freelance work for an advertising agency to create an ad for vodka from Kazakhstan. We found it hard; the problem was the product, which had a long unpronounceable name and an old-fashioned bottle. Usually the agency advertised the product the client gave them without question, but in this case we ignored the usual rules and redesigned the product so we could advertise it better. We went back to them with a new bottle, a new name, and of course an ad to promote the vodka. How will you change your product, if it doesn't work? What will you add or remove?

2   What do you want to change? What annoys you? Be like Darwin and embrace hacking as a way of thinking about everything you encounter. If Darwin thought a standard medical treatment didn't work, as a trained doctor, he'd improve it to make it more effective.

Make the future now

New developments jump out at us more and more quickly. The speed of change increases; new jobs spring up while others become obsolete; something that was new yesterday is already outdated today. We're so busy dealing with new ideas, we forget to create our own.

Predict the future of your field and detect upcoming developments. Imagine how you'd like the future to be, then go about shaping and creating it. This will give your work value into the distant future and prevent it becoming obsolete.

Raymond Loewy was impatient to see the future, so he got there before anyone else. He revolutionized the design industry by predicting design twenty to thirty years ahead, and from the 1920s, he built the future with a new streamlined style suggesting speed and technological innovation. Loewy was known as 'the Man Who Shaped America' because he designed everything from lipsticks to locomotives – Lucky Strike cigarette packets, NASA spacecraft, Studebakers, refrigerators, Greyhound buses, and the Coke bottle. Nothing was too big or too small. He transformed banal objects and gave them an iconic, magical aura.

Is it a bird? Is it a plane? Is it a rocket? No, it's a pencil sharpener. Sharpening a pencil became an event with Loewy's futuristic pencil sharpener of 1934. He must have felt at home in the world because when he looked around at trains, cars and kitchen appliances, either he had designed them or someone had copied his style. He stayed relevant throughout his life by always being a step ahead, predicting the future of each object and then creating it.

Is it a bird? Is it a plane? Is it a . . .

Are you bogged down in admin? Imagine admin in thirty years. Get to the future before anyone else. Be the person everyone has to catch. Don't become trapped in 'now' – always look to the future. The primary function of the neo-cortex is prediction; it's the essential attribute of the human mind and gives us an advantage over other animals. Examine every aspect of your field and predict how it will be in ten years, then create it. Predicting the future will force you to be more inventive, and it raises everyone's aspirations. Maybe you don't like what you see around you – you want it to be more ethical, inclusive or sustainable. Then it's down to you to create an alternative.

Banks, hospitals and insurance companies call me in for advice because they are good at repeating what has been successful in the past but very poor at thinking far ahead.

They solve today's problems when they should be anticipating future difficulties and creating future solutions.

1   Be impatient to see the future before it happens. Look for the latest trends and developments and analyse how they could evolve further. What would be the ideal future? Think of yourself as the person to create utopia.

2   Create the job of the future. Either be entrepreneurial like a businessman or an artist, or create a new position in your company. New job roles appear all the time. If you don't like your job and there are no others available, create a new post.

3   Learn skills that can transfer from one industry to another. Leadership, creativity, communication and innovation are skills for the jobs of tomorrow. A nurse with business skills, a fund manager with creative thinking skills, or an administrator with entrepreneurial abilities will be more employable.

It's not what you look at – it's what you see

Most of the time, we look at things but don't see them. Looking is casual. Seeing is about being perceptive. Input from our eyes is data, and perception is analysing the information. We must use our mind's eye and not just our physical sight.

The passenger in a car sees many things the driver doesn't notice. Most of us overlook fantastic opportunities sitting under our noses. Seeing is the art of noticing what is invisible to everyone else; develop an eye for seeing the brilliant in the mundane, and a whole world of inspiration opens up. You have to work hard at seeing – it might feel as if it's something you do naturally, but it requires constant awareness.

Designer Aarish Netarwala noticed a long queue had formed on a beach in California. A massive crowd of athletes was waiting for the chance to exercise on steep dunes. Their feet sank into the sand, making running strenuous and creating the ultimate workout. Netarwala responded to the demand by creating the extraordinary Grit Adidas trainer – a shoe with a built-in dune. A unique lattice sole makes the foot unstable on impact with the ground, as if the wearer is sinking into soft sand.

Extraordinary opportunities are staring us in the face every day, but we don't notice. Most people are too preoccupied to see the overlooked, but successful people work hard at seeing. Don't look for anything in particular; just see. Everyone walks past many potentially brilliant opportunities every day. Great creative people notice and respond to them. 'Anytime you see duct tape in the world, that's a design opportunity,' said Airbnb co-founder Joe Gebbia on the TED Radio Hour.

Looking is passive; seeing is active. We have to train ourselves to look deeply and interrogate everything. Pieter's fame was due to his ability to understand people's drives and motivations. He put on a disguise and slipped into a wedding reception, uninvited. The record of his observations would have a lasting effect that even he could not have imagined. Pieter pretended to know the newlywed couple and joined in the fun and dancing, but he was investigating, talking to the guests and digging into their lives.

The concealment paid off when he produced a revealing image of the event, *The Wedding Dance*. In it, a crowd of drunken revellers flirt, dance and chatter, and Pieter captured the dancers' spirit of playfulness and wild abandon.

The Wedding Dance is an oil painting produced by Pieter Bruegel the Elder in 1566. Bruegel's biographer Karel van Mander wrote, 'Bruegel would often go outside to join the Peasants, at their Fairs, and at their Weddings, dressed up as a Peasant, giving gifts like the other guests, pretending to belong to the bride's or the groom's family or people. Bruegel rejoiced in doing so, being among the Peasants, eating, drinking, dancing . . .' Bruegel packed the painting with so many characters and keenly observed scenes that you can return repeatedly to the painting and discover new incidents each time.

In sixteenth-century Holland, dance was regulated by strict rules of conduct because the ruling elite and the church authorities considered it a source of evil. The middle and upper classes adhered to rigid codes of behaviour, and Bruegel loved the peasants' sense of freedom from social standards and the way the country folk were in touch with their instincts. His love for ordinary people shines through in his visual description of the rustic charm and warm atmosphere of the occasion.

As with dance, oil painting was governed by strict, socially accepted rules and confined to grandiose subjects like religion, mythology and the lives of great men. Bruegel's paintings opened the floodgates. By showing the quirks of everyday human life, Bruegel enlarged the range of subjects, and artists began to explore previously forbidden themes and topics.

1 Develop the ability to see deeply. It's essential in fields as diverse as physics, all the arts, and the media. Scientists from astrophysicists to chemists are observers. The more deeply they observe, the less they miss. The same is true of artists, people in business – in every industry, in fact. It's a critical skill for all students in the twenty-first century. Not enough time is devoted to developing students' ability to see deeper.

2   Be prepared to do whatever it takes to research and dig deep into your subject. I was asked by an NHS surgeon to determine why so many patients complained that their hospital experience was substandard, when the hospital's investigations proved it was excellent. I asked the surgeon to live out the patient experience. He was reluctant at first but eventually lay on a trolley. The first experience was being admitted without any explanation of what was about to happen. Then he lay in a corridor for half an hour, staring at the strip lights. For the first time, he saw things from the patient's perspective. Explaining something doesn't get the message across as well as experiencing it. The surgeon suddenly understood the patients' problems and could see the solutions.

Give your work personality – your personality

Does your work reflect your personality? If not, it's not your work.

As a child, Alberto hated his grandfather's 'grey, dark and boring' factory, founded in 1921. His grandfather, a skilled metalsmith, produced functional, traditional kitchen utensils. The atmosphere was dour and drab, whereas Alberto was playful and irreverent. He dreaded having to join the family business and when the time finally arrived, he rebelled. He commissioned Salvador Dalí to design a completely new kitchen utensil. His grandfather hated the idea, but Alberto insisted. Dalí's device was so unusual that no one could work out what it did and, perhaps because of language difficulties, Dalí couldn't explain. It's in a museum now, and still no one knows. It was a commercial disaster, but the idea of getting artists and designers to infuse ordinary objects with their personality was born. Alberto changed the factory with his fun-loving, irreverent character. His designers transformed humble, everyday items like egg cups, cheese graters and pepper grinders into delightful, engaging objects. It was a masterstroke because it made Alberto's company, Alessi, stand out from the competition. A brand's personality influences the public's emotional response to a company's product or service.

Alessi commissioned the witty, elegant and playful Kettle 9093 that reflected designer Michael Graves' irreverent and playful personality. Kettle 9093 made a mundane task fun: when the water boiled, the bird in the spout sang. The public was entranced. It became a design icon and continues to sell hundreds of thousands a year. Graves showed how a small, humdrum domestic item could be fun and also prestigious. People in authority wondered: if he could make a great, standout kettle, what could he do with a big project? Thanks to the kettle's reputation, Graves received commissions to design important buildings that, crucially, also reflected his playful personality.

Tweet, tweet, tweet

Graves' success proved the value of 'designer' objects to Alessi, and they emphasized the personality of the designer. It wasn't just a kettle; it was a Michael Graves kettle. Don't just create an object or service, make a character of it in the same way an animator would. Who are they? People react to objects, houses, websites and organizations like Nike that have a personality. We like to think our decisions are logical and sensible, but we're deluding ourselves – we make decisions with our hearts first, then later think them over in our minds. Personality makes your product or service memorable.

Alberto's dedication to playfulness and good design took off when he commissioned designers and architects who had never created industrial design products to rethink how everyday objects could work. The company has been responsible for a vast number of design classics and has an annual turnover of £100 million.

Most of our work looks like everyone else's work. Make your project personal, and you'll make it special and unique – even a minor project can have a significant impact if you throw your personality into it. Character is a mysterious power that draws you to some people and repels you from others. Personality affects our choices, so it's essential to use it to attract people to your work.

I delivered a creative thinking workshop for a company that bought and sold millions of tons of grain. I assumed their business would be all about profit margins, net losses, outgoing costs and other financial dealings. But it surprised me to discover that the company's customers were loyal because they liked them and found them trustworthy. It was the company's personality, not good deals that made them popular with other businesses. People buy into brands, artists, writers, musicians if they can relate to their personality: Jackson Pollock's paintings are lively and agitated – like him; Dostoyevsky's novels are deeply philosophical – like him; Dietrich Mateschitz is a high-energy personality who enjoys travelling the world and piloting his planes – and he poured his character into his energy drink, Red Bull.

Alessi transformed a dreary, dull factory into a business worth tens of millions by injecting personality into it from the products to the brand itself. It's the most comfortable and cheapest way to give your work a standout, lasting appeal.

Put your personality into your work because it gives your work personality. 'I am me all day. It's quite a responsibility,' said singer–songwriter Morrissey. But it's what makes his work so unique and special. When you finish a project, look at it and ask yourself, 'Is it me?' What is your personality? Is your work infused with it?

1 What are the main features of your personality? Look at your work and ask yourself if those features are coming through – if not, you need to ask why not?

2 Recall the last person you met who was charming and fascinating. What was it about their personality that pulled you to them? You got on with them and formed an emotional connection. Perhaps they were a laugh, or you felt you could be open with them. You quickly considered them a friend. Think of your work as a personality that creates an emotional connection to others.

What you hate helps you understand what you love

Sometimes it's hard to work out what you really want to do. We often suffer from 'decision paralysis': there are so many possible courses we could take, it's hard to know where to begin.

Work out what you would most hate to do. Then do the exact opposite.

In 1980, a group of designers were invited to have an exhibition. They were all enthusiastic about the big opportunity, but they argued for hours about a theme and couldn't agree on anything. Eventually one designer, Ettore Sottsass, suggested they define what they hated. Suddenly, everything became easier and clearer. They were united in their hatred of the oppressively rational rules of modernism – no colour! No ornamentation! No fun! They met up later with ideas that were the exact opposite of modernism and their new, untamed, vigorous furniture designs were revolutionary. No colour became bright colours. Rational became irrational. Functional became playful. Matt finishes became shiny. Plain surfaces became flamboyantly patterned. They had fun, made everyday objects fun and brought fun to anyone who owned their work. A world of possibilities opened up and led to the phrase 'form follows fun', a subversion of the po-faced modernist mantra, 'form follows function'. Their exhibition caused a sensation and blew away the rules of design. What started out as a criticism went down in the history of design as a style called Memphis, the first postmodern movement.

Find the things you most hate. Find a designer or writer whose work you hate and work out exactly why you hate it. Make a list of things you would most hate to create yourself – then create the opposite. It will give you an insight into your values.

If you hate something, it's because you care about it. Therapists tell patients to let go of negative feelings and forgive people or things they hate, but in the creative world, that feeling of hate can give you an insight. As Carl Jung said, 'Everything that irritates us about others can lead us to an understanding of ourselves.' The apathetic feel nothing. What you want to destroy tells you what you want to create.

I'm sure you've had that feeling when a song, a book, a film or whatever is hugely popular and you wonder, how could anyone like this rubbish? You feel disappointment in your fellow man. Why does this rubbish have an exhibition at the Tate, why is this book number one in the non-fiction charts? You feel that nothing makes sense; the values of the world are ones you can't relate to. But it's a good thing to react to.

An unknown young man called Ian walked through the backstreets of his home town of Salford. Everywhere he went, an irritating, saccharine, bland song called 'Love Will Keep Us Together' by Captain and Tennille seeped out of cafés, shops and passing car radios. *Billboard* magazine rated it the biggest hit of 1975, with more weeks at number one than any other song. Ian hated soft rock, but it dominated the mid-70s. Salford was an apocalyptic cityscape of urban decay, smashed windows, rusting cranes in the abandoned docks and everything covered in a thin layer of soot, and the saccharine song sounded ridiculous and represented everything Ian hated. He was so incensed by its success that it was a catalyst. Infuriated and believing that music didn't have to be like this manufactured abomination, Ian Curtis, the lead singer of Joy Division, set out to put things right and give the world some real, human, relevant music. He turned his despair into action and wrote a song that was the exact opposite. The title was his starting point.

Captain and Tennille 'Love Will Keep Us Together'	Ian Curtis/Joy Division 'Love Will Tear Us Apart'
Lyrics: bland, clichéd and shallow, 'You belong to me now, ain't gonna set you free now.'	Lyrics: personal, poetic and haunting with a deep insight into a relationship. 'And we're changing our ways, taking different roads.'
Sound: soft, schmaltzy and overproduced.	Sound: raw, urgent, with slashing metal guitars and minimal production.
Cover art: a photo of Captain and Tennille looking healthy and tanned with perfectly coiffured hair. They smile showing perfect white teeth while cuddling puppies.	Cover art: a photo created by etching the song title onto a sheet of metal, ageing it with acid and leaving it outside to make it look like a weathered stone slab. On the 12-inch version there is a photograph of a grieving angel in an Italian cemetery.
Relationships: Captain and Tennille went on to have a forty-year marriage.	Relationships: Curtis was in the process of breaking up with his partner.

Success: 'Love Will Keep Us Together' reached number one and was the biggest hit of the year, but is largely forgotten.

Success: 'Love Will Tear Us Apart' struggled to number 13 in the UK charts, but became a timeless, legendary classic.

Insiders: Captain and Tennille worked with the biggest names in show business for years and knew everyone important. They hosted their own family-friendly, TV variety show.

Outsiders: Ian Curtis was totally unknown. He suffered from anxiety and was diagnosed with medical problems such as epilepsy. He lived in Salford, a post-industrial wasteland far from the cultural centre of London.

1   What you hate defines you as much as what you love. Hate can clarify and motivate. Hate tells you who you are and your values; it tells you what you care about. What you hate about your job could lead to you creating a new entrepreneurial position.

2   Respond constructively to your feelings of anger. Hatred tells you what you will not stand for, so use that knowledge to change things and replace what you hate.

Slash at your work – before someone else does

Being criticized is painful, so get your retaliation in first. Take a knife to it yourself – before anyone else gets the chance. Be the severest critic of your work. Edit ruthlessly. Leave nothing weak for others to pick on.

Alfred Hitchcock proudly showed the newly finished version of his film *Psycho* at a special screening to executives at Paramount Pictures. The film ended, and they sat in stunned silence. They were horrified: it was the most boring film they'd ever seen. The only suspense they'd felt was 'When will it end?' They decided not to release it as a film but reluctantly agreed it might make a mediocre TV drama. Now it was Hitchcock who was horrified –

this decision was a dagger to his heart. He thought *Psycho* was important enough to be released in cinemas and, feeling desperate, he withdrew into himself for a few days. When he emerged, he ruthlessly slashed at the film with a knife – in the editing suite.

Using all his skills as an editor, Hitchcock transformed *Psycho* into something brilliant. He ruthlessly cut it up, editing and re-editing repeatedly. Eventually, Paramount agreed to distribute the new version in cinemas and it became Hitchcock's most significant success. He had made an almost infinite number of versions of *Psycho* – the boring one and hundreds of others.

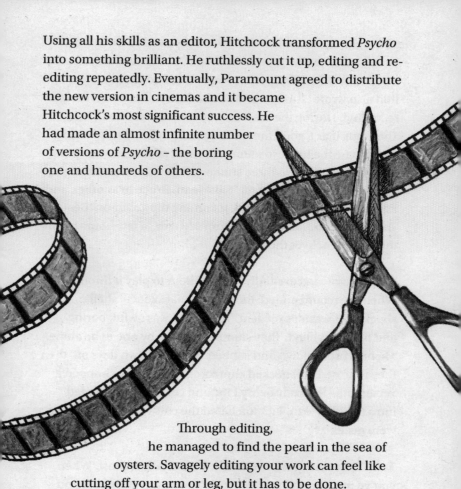

Through editing, he managed to find the pearl in the sea of oysters. Savagely editing your work can feel like cutting off your arm or leg, but it has to be done.

Thriller was Michael Jackson's eagerly awaited follow-up to *Off the Wall*. Jackson was so disappointed he'd only won one Grammy for *Off the Wall* that he shut himself in his room for days. He wanted *Thriller* to be brilliant. But it was behind schedule with two months left until the record company's deadline, so the production team – Michael, songwriter Rod Temperton, the great engineer Bruce Swedien – worked day and night. Bruce told Michael that they needed a black rock 'n' roll tune, and he produced 'Beat It'. Bruce said they needed a ballad and Rod Temperton wrote 'The Lady in My Life'. Rod also wrote 'Thriller' and Michael threw his heart into its recording. During the session, a speaker burst into flames. They took it as a good omen. They were right: *Thriller* would go on to be the highest-selling album of all time. At one point they were working in three studios at the same time all night, Michael in one, working on 'Billie Jean', Bruce in another, and Eddie Van Halen in the third, recording the guitar on 'Beat It'. They finally completed the album at 9 a.m., a few hours before they had to deliver the pressing.

They all crowded excitedly into Studio A to play it through. When the record ended, they sat in total silence, shell-shocked. It wasn't excellent. The sound was awful, boring, and nothing gelled. They slumped off one by one to be alone. Michael broke down and sobbed. They took two days off, then they returned and hacked chunks out of it – they chopped a verse from 'The Lady in My Life' and cut out the extended intro to 'Billie Jean'. Jackson hated the cuts but accepted they were necessary.

1 Edit your work ruthlessly. Be brutally honest. When you've put hours into your work, you're too close to it and can't judge if it's any good. It's painful to cut out chunks you spent hours lovingly crafting but you're holding on to it for the wrong reasons. You're not holding on to it because it's brilliant.

2 What is vague, muddled or sluggish? Can this part be justified? Have I confused people with too much information? Is the message clear? Is this the best it can be?

3   You can transform something mediocre into something brilliant with editing. Attack your work before your audience wounds you. It's painful, but less painful than being attacked by others.

Make the impossible possible

What do you do when you've tried everything you can think of to solve a problem, but it still seems impossible to fix? If a task seems unsolvable, it's because your thinking is wrong. Chances are, you're using conventional approaches to an unconventional problem. Think alternatively, and new, better solutions appear.

Some people make possible a task others have dismissed as impossible. The challenges of a demanding task bring out your qualities more than something that's easily attainable. You must resolve to be more ingenious – focus on the options, not on the limitations.

Architects believed a small plot of land in Brazil was impossible to build on. The plot consisted of two small areas split between an old factory chimney and a nineteenth-century factory with an underground stream flowing through the middle – an architect's nightmare. They tried to tackle it in the way they had always done, but they became stuck on the many problems, and they froze. It seemed impossible because they were trying to put a conventional building on an unconventional location.

Architect Lina Bo Bardi found a way to build a sports and culture centre on it by stacking the swimming pools and basketball courts on top of each other on one area, and layering the changing rooms in a tower on the other –

and connecting them with flying bridges. She transformed an impossible plot into an exciting mix of architectural imagination and social utopianism, which became the SESC Pompéia. Given a standard site, she'd probably have produced a conventional building, and I wouldn't be writing about her. Positive beliefs are powerful. Do what is possible. Build tall towers where you can build tall towers. Connect them however possible. Other designers focused on what wasn't possible, but Lina Bo Bardi concentrated on what was.

Conventional thinking can be a trap when faced with an unusual problem, and our perception of a situation can be a source of weakness rather than a source of strength. Put aside all the prejudices, noise and fears in your head and see a situation with fresh eyes: you will see things for what they are when everyone else is looking through the fog of their training, prejudices and assumptions.

Alec Issigonis was nicknamed 'the Greek god' by his contemporaries because he performed miracles. In the late 1950s, governments severely rationed fuel because of the Suez Crisis and Issigonis's company gave him an impossible task: to make a car significantly smaller but hugely increase the space for passengers. He responded by tearing the conventions of car design apart: he put the engine sideways. It increased the area inside, but made the car shorter and perfect for city life. The result, the Mini, is the highest-selling British car in history and is still in production today. It's the most influential car of all time because turning the engine sideways forced other groundbreaking innovations: a sump gearbox, 10-inch wheels, and the most innovative of all, a front-wheel drive. Issigonis ignored the people who told him it was impossible and went on to produce magic. Instead of letting the problem cloud his thinking, he considered the unthinkable.

Early one morning, two of my third-year students went for a job interview at one of the world's top advertising agencies. They were a team, copywriter and art director, and presented their portfolio. Their work was brilliant, and the interviewers were astonished and excited by their ads. But at the end of the interview, they were told, 'Your work is brilliant, and we'd like to hire you, but you're too young and you don't have enough experience, so come back in three or four years when you're older.' They returned to college at lunchtime, crushed. Their work was mature, but they weren't deemed old enough. It seemed like an insurmountable problem, but we dyed their hair grey, dressed them in old-fashioned clothes, painted lines on their faces, and sent them straight back to the agency in the afternoon. They asked to see their interviewers and declared, 'We're old enough now.' They were hired on the spot.

1   Search for possibilities in a seemingly impossible task, and alternative thinking will uncover opportunities you overlooked. A mother had complications giving birth. The obstetricians used forceps and accidentally severed a nerve in the baby's face, causing paralysis in his tongue, chin and half of his lip. He grew up with a permanently snarling expression and slurred speech. But he wanted to be an actor. He overcame the obstacle by writing a film script with a part for himself as a boxer. *Rocky* made Sylvester Stallone one of the most iconic actors of his generation. Search for what is possible and build on those foundations; craft your idea around what is doable.

2   Don't listen to the doubters and the negativity of others. Most worthwhile endeavours seem impossible at some point – until you harness your imagination's power to overcome them. Born a slave, Frederick Douglass was separated from his parents and lived a life of suffering and violence. The pro-slavery elite argued slaves did not have the intellectual ability to live as independent American citizens, so Douglass made himself into a living counterexample. He taught himself to read and became the anti-slavery movement's leader due to his persuasive oratory and incisive writing. His task seemed impossible to others but, he realized, set out to prove the doubters wrong, and you'll find you're doing the impossible.

Expand your role

If we're not careful, people have a fixed view of our capabilities; they pigeonhole us into a role, and we're trapped. It's hard to make people see you in a different or a more significant position. If you're low in your sphere, it's easy to feel overlooked and neglected. But there are ways to make a substantial contribution and put yourself centre stage. That decision alone sets you on your way. To expand your role, you'll need to be resourceful and imaginative.

Julius Neubronner was a pigeon fancier. The German military recruited him to use homing pigeons to deliver messages during the First World War, but it was a frustratingly marginal role. He wanted to be at the centre of things and make a significant contribution. An idea hatched in his mind and he invented a miniature camera with a harness to attach to pigeons, and a timer to trigger the shutter at set intervals. His pigeons would photograph enemy positions. He pitched the idea to the top brass, but they weren't interested – it wasn't a bigger gun, a new warship or a missile. To them, he was just a pigeon fancier, and they didn't take him seriously. Neubronner ignored them and went ahead with his idea. His photographs revealed the exact locations of enemy positions, their tanks, and the number of personnel, artillery and resources. His bird's-eye view proved the importance of aerial reconnaissance, and with the photographic evidence in front of them, the Germans meticulously planned attacks. The top brass suddenly changed their view of Neubronner, and he soared from a mere pigeon supervisor to the provider of crucial military surveillance. Now, the generals waited for Neubronner's information before they made a decision. He transformed the future of battle and made reconnaissance an essential component.

Anyone in a minor position with limited opportunities can grow his or her role. Don't expect help from your superiors, though – they're happy with their more significant role, and with you being in a minor position. It's down to you to raise yourself and turn your project from an ugly duckling into a swan. The abilities that got you to your present position will not get you to the next stage.

Actress Sharon Stone accepted a small part in Martin Scorsese's film *Casino*. The character was blonde, beautiful and shallow. But she didn't merely take the script, memorize and then perform the role. She kept suggesting ways to expand her character and proposed extra lines, scenes and subplots. She transformed her limited role into one of significance and depth, going on to win an Academy Award nomination, a

Golden Globe, and crucially made the film industry recognize her as a serious actress. If you have a small role, think about how you can expand it.

In one of my workshops, a student explained she felt trapped in her role as an IT technician for a car manufacturer. Like a lot of talented people, she was brilliant at her work but terrible at interviews. She had to wait for a position to become available, apply, and then go through the interview process. But in a company, it's hard to progress if you're no good at interviews. In the workshop, we suggested she created an entirely new role for herself. She started up courses within the company to mentor managers and show them how to use online technology and media more effectively. Things went well. She got to know the leaders, and they expanded her role. She soon dropped IT and began managing a division, and from there she went from strength to strength. Don't wait for a purpose. Make it. When you've made it, expand it.

How to make decisions more decisively

Making the right decisions is difficult – but crucial. The wrong decision, even the smallest, can send your project or your career off track. Out of the enormous number of choices we face, it's essential to know which lead to success and which to failure. We are the creative directors of our lives, and through our decisions we achieve our goals. Fortunately, there's a way to be sure that those decisions are the right ones.

Every choice you make makes you. It's essential to establish what matters to you, and that must become the core of your work. What is the deeper substance of your venture? What is the theme underpinning everything in the project? Knowing your topic ensures you make the right decisions. If you have a lapse of concentration at the beginning of a project, it's hard to recover. Many of the clients I work for have a 'we'll sort it out later' attitude. They are about to spend months working on something, but they rush ahead without establishing what is at the root of their project. The theme has to be something deep and meaningful to you personally, to make the tough decisions easier.

Film director Francis Ford Coppola explained why a one-word theme is essential: 'In *The Godfather*, it was succession. In *The Conversation*, it was privacy. In *Apocalypse*, it was morality.' The life of a director or any creative person is about making a host of decisions, quickly. Coppola continues, 'In *The Conversation*, they brought all these coats to me, and they said: Do you want him to look like a detective, [like] Humphrey Bogart? Do you want him to look like a blah blah blah? I didn't know, and said the theme is "privacy" and chose the plastic coat you could see through. So knowing the theme helps you make a decision when you're not sure which way to go.'

A goal is what you want to achieve, but the theme is what is important to you. Your goal can seem a long way off, but your theme makes you excited to jump out of bed early in the morning. Get to the heart of what you're doing by asking yourself 'why is this important to me?' Sum up your theme in one word because it gives you direction and makes moving forward easier for you and everyone else.

I had simultaneous feelings of delight and recklessness as I stood on the top floor of Palazzo Strozzi in Florence and looked down at the daunting drop of 20 metres. I took a deep breath and pushed myself off. The walls and Corinthian columns of the Strozzi flew past in a colourful jumble; I picked up speed and wanted to scream, but I was travelling so fast I couldn't make a sound. After a few seconds, I was overwhelmed by a lightheaded delirium of adrenaline when I struck the floor. I had just hurtled down 50 metres of giant see-through pirouetting tubing, an interactive sculpture by artist Carsten Höller. The theme of all Höller's work is 'relationships'. Höller uses his training as a scientist to communicate ideas about the nature of human relationships, and reacts to the formal urban spaces we live in by creating liberating work that encourages us to 'let go'. His *Golden Mirror Carousel* from 2014 is a life-size replica of a fairground carousel, made of gold mirrors. It turns the art gallery into an amusement park and breaks down barriers between people. Höller uses many different mediums, but his life's work is coherent and held together by having a constant theme.

1   What's your theme? Nothing is as straightforward as you expect. Problems regularly arise that could derail a project, so a central topic keeps you on course when distractions and people are trying to lead you astray. I've learned from writing four books to have a clear theme before I start; this book's was to help people achieve their ambition to produce brilliant work.

2   Sum your theme up in one sentence so that you can remind anyone involved in the project of what it is. A topic helps keep you on track and is a foundation for your project. Your theme is like a friend who sticks by your side, advising and supporting you.

Discover what makes you flow

Too often, someone has a great idea, then they plan and prepare for months. They anticipate everything that could go wrong, but in doing so they lose their energy and enthusiasm, the project goes stale and they give up. Once you start a project, aim to produce it instantly – don't stop till it's finished. Brilliant work is created in a state called 'flow': the complete, unconditional immersion in what you're doing. Solve problems as you work. You're at your best when your body and mind are stretched to their limits to achieve a difficult task. You're completely absorbed in the mission, alert, unselfconscious, at the peak of your performance and so involved that nothing else matters, not even time and food. Avoid distractions that disrupt this state. There are five steps you need to create flow, which we'll come to later.

Can you remember the last time you were so engrossed in your work that time stood still? If it wasn't yesterday, something is wrong. Athletes call it being 'in the zone' and creative people call it 'flow'. Psychologists believe it is essential for a meaningful experience. The purpose of 'flow' is to put your worldly concerns to one side so you can concentrate on a higher goal. The ancient Chinese philosopher Lao Tzu, writing in the *Tao Te Ching*, called it 'doing without doing'. It's the state when our best work appears without struggle or agitation.

Edwin Land invented instant film in 1947 and only a year later unveiled the first commercial instant camera – the Polaroid. He struggled with scientific development because he didn't have a laboratory, but he found a solution. In those days, security was lax at universities and he discovered he could sneak into a Columbia University laboratory during the night and use their equipment. When Land finally had the finance for his workshop, he worked ceaselessly while teams of assistants supported him in shifts. When one team felt worn out, they were replaced by the next to enable him to work continuously and not break his flow. Land wouldn't let anything deflect his attention. Assistants delivered his meals and pressurized him to eat. He once wore the same clothes for over two weeks to avoid leaving his work and breaking the flow. He had no concept of time. He didn't know when it was dinner time, lunch, day or night. Standard time meant nothing to him because he was in the time zone of the project. If you're conscious of time – that your project should take a month, six months, or however long – you start to rush and cut corners. Land wasn't in a hurry, but he wasn't taking any time off either – he applied himself. He tried one option after another until something worked.

Bringing a project to completion is a struggle and you have to enjoy the difficulties and feed off them. If you're trying to make something that's never existed before, it will be challenging.

You have to be persistent but also resistant to interruption and distraction. You have to decide you're in it for the long haul. When you have an idea, be relentless and make it happen quickly. If you procrastinate, a committee meets in your head, analyses the problem and overthinks it, then self-doubt creeps in, obstacles seem insurmountable, your energy fades and your interest fades. Don't pause for thought; think while you're making. Land didn't go on holiday, have weekend breaks or long lunches. When he started the project, he worked until he finished the camera. If you're distracted, you can't achieve great success. Concentrate on the things that matter most in life, and ignore the things that don't help you. It's only a dream for a short time before you make it a reality.

1   Clear mental chaos. Whatever's preoccupying your mind that stops you from achieving flow, resolve it. Decide what task you're going to do today – then do it no matter what. The average person spends almost thirty hours a week watching TV. Imagine if they spent that time making or creating something.

2   Shut out all interruption. It would be best if you had total concentration to get in the zone. It's what the painter William Blake meant when he said, 'I myself do nothing. The Holy Spirit accomplishes all through me.'

3 To find your flow, you need the right environment. I wrote the structure of this chapter in the canteen during my lunch break during a day's teaching at Central Saint Martins. The atmosphere of energy, youth and innovation from the students rubbed off on me. But I then had to sit quietly in my studio and write for hours until the chapter's elements fell into place. 'The age in which we live, this non-stop distraction, is making it more impossible for the young generation to ever have the curiosity or discipline because you need to be alone to find out anything,' said Vivienne Westwood.

4 Put aside plenty of time. If you're hurrying, you can't lose yourself in the flow.

5 Don't censor yourself. Suspend judgment. Shut out your self-critic and completely open your mind. Don't get feedback until you've finished, or doubters will sap your energy.

Help people to help you

A huge snowball picked up speed as it rolled along, with the people it crashed into becoming cemented to it. The snowball collided with an assistant film director who stuck and rolled along with it. Then it rolled into an agent, a producer, a cinematographer and many others, all of whom became cemented. The snowball was Robert Altman, one of the greatest and most influential film directors of his generation. He was nominated for five best director Academy Awards and as he moved from one film to another, others with an equally strong drive to create brilliant films stayed with him. He gave them freedom and urged them to fulfil their potential. He was the cement that held a team together, and he became the director everyone wanted to work for. Being involved in a brilliant film advanced everyone's careers.

We are more inclined to ask for help in areas where our ego is not involved. We'll take a car to a garage if it breaks down, but if a painting goes badly wrong we're reluctant to ask a friend for feedback. We feel it's admitting defeat to ask for help – but asking for help is a skill.

You can't produce brilliant work without help from others. It's counterintuitive, but the more generous you are, the more people give you. A script is words on paper; to bring it to life on film requires a huge, passionate team. If you're an artist you'll need a gallery owner, collectors and critics on your side. An entrepreneur needs customers and associates to help them along. I need an agent, editor, publisher, bookseller and you. I have to convince all of you this book is worth being involved in. If people see you want to produce something brilliant, they'll join in with you – everyone wants to be part of something exceptional. Be the person who provides it for them.

You need those around you to be enthusiastic and energized. Different things motivate different people, and not everyone is motivated solely by money or recognition. Work out what motivates them and you can help give them the right incentive to get involved. You can help them fulfil their ambitions, and help you in return. We tend to go into things thinking about what we want, but be sensitive to what others want too.

Think of a party host. They walk around offering bowls of crisps or presenting drinks and introducing people to each other. Make sure everyone engaged with your project is feeling fulfilled. Whoever you're working with – a website designer, photographer, graphic designer or whoever – motivate them to help you produce brilliant work. They are a river of ideas and you need to help them flow.

Whenever the great film director and screenwriter John Cassavetes made a movie, he led a huge film crew. He said, 'In directing you're really like a host, [in] that everyone's going to your party, and it's very difficult for the crew to help you get glory. Once they trust that you really are interested in the work, and not in your own perfection, they will work very hard for you.' He always put the crew at ease and made sure they were all having fun. Cassavetes' films were nominated for numerous Academy Awards and pioneered the use of improvisation and *cinéma vérité* – realistic, documentary-style films with no artificial or artistic effects. When you work with others, it's important to lead by example, and Cassavetes was a non-directing director. He encouraged everyone on the set to improvise and suggest ideas and this was the key to his success: making people want to contribute to making a brilliant film.

Some film directors are so busy giving orders and telling everyone what they want that they forget to listen. Try to talk less and listen more attentively. We are all the directors of our work, but we need collaboration. It's easy to fall into the trap of telling people off for doing something wrong rather than inspiring them to do great work. Pointing out what's wrong is easier than pointing out how to put things right.

To get brilliant results you must share, inspire and spread your passion. Being egotistical or arrogant won't motivate others to help you produce brilliant work; it'll do the opposite. Create a domino effect: enthuse someone and they'll enthuse the next person down the line and so on. Your task is to unlock the potential of others, who in turn will help your work be brilliant. Inspire people to do better and you'll do better.

When I deliver workshops to The Future Group, I try to instil in them 'shared control' principles. If you have an 'I lead, you follow' attitude, everyone takes a back seat because someone else is driving. But you need everyone to stay alert and involved. Try to share control and switch leadership back and forth so that everyone takes responsibility. Doing what needs to be done should be your overriding consideration. Whenever I have tried this approach as a consultant, everyone focuses on achieving what is most important.

In recent years I've been fortunate to be asked into hospitals to deliver creative thinking workshops. Many of their problems are not the result of negligence, but of small oversights such as a doctor forgetting to remind a nurse about a treatment, a nurse unable to read a doctor's handwriting, or a bottle labelled obscurely. We have the best doctors, nurses and hospitals in the world; all their efforts are directed to patient care. But accountants and office administrators who care about numbers on spreadsheets run hospitals. The doctors and nurses are not cared for but treated like statistics. Consequently they feel alienated from the organization and it impacts on their work. This is brought into sharp focus for me in my work with them, because the result of this lack of care is needless death. My time is spent trying to convince the hospital to care for their staff as much as they do for their patients. To make their employees feel valued.

1   Be sensitive to the needs of others. Support them by making them aware that their contribution is invaluable. It's only fair that they get something out of your project, because they have needs and ambitions too.

2   Sometimes it takes courage to let others have a say in your work. Take risks, and it encourages others to take risks. Acknowledge that risk-taking could lead to short-term failures and that's OK, because in the long run it will lead to greater success.

How to work faster and smarter – stretch yourself

In the 80s, I thought I was doing well. I left the Royal College of Art and had two successful one-person exhibitions at a gallery in London's heart. They sold out with the help of critically acclaimed reviews by Edward Lucie-Smith in *The Times*. It took me about a year to produce enough paintings for an exhibition – the standard time for most professional artists.

Some of my friends had stayed in New York for a few weeks and become friends with a young American artist. He came over to England because he had been offered an exhibition in a prestigious London gallery, the Institute of Contemporary Art. I went along to the private view and chatted with him; he was softly spoken, seemed insecure, and repeatedly asked what I thought of his sixteen large paintings. I was astonished to discover that the whole exhibition had taken him only a few days to put together – an extraordinarily short time. His New York gallery flew him over to London, set him up in a rented studio, and he worked day and night to finish the paintings on time. The exhibition opened, he attended the private view, then flew off to repeat the process at his next show in Zürich. By having the paintings made in London, his dealer avoided customs and the cost of shipping them over, and he pre-sold the paintings to London galleries for US$20,000 each before the artist had even painted them. This money paid for the trip. His schedule was relentless. He stepped out of his comfort zone so often that he was never actually in it, but he found a way to work quickly and maintain high quality and he directed every ounce of his energy towards the next exhibition – not just the paintings, but also the logistics and difficulties that inevitably arise. I'd never heard of Jean-Michel Basquiat until his ICA exhibition. Still, he became one of his generation's great artists, and any of those paintings are now worth over US$100 million.

Basquiat and I were roughly the same age. I had a one-person exhibition every year – yet he was having up to eight a year. He realized he was one of tens of thousands of artists globally, and to stand out, he'd have to throw everything he had at his career. I realized I was working well within my comfort zone, and I re-examined myself and my process. I started working on a bigger scale, with more concentration and faster.

You achieve brilliant work by stretching yourself beyond what you think is possible. Assess what you're capable of, then reach beyond it. You only achieve real growth in art, business and life if you set yourself a goal beyond your reach. To make the best use of your time, work faster and more efficiently while maintaining the highest quality. Be more prolific. Produce more in a shorter space of time.

My book, *Ideas Are Your Only Currency*, explains the importance of working hard and fast to get ideas. It contains one hundred projects to produce in five days, roughly ten minutes per project, without using the internet or library.

1   Stretch yourself. People work faster and smarter if they create a personalized structure to their day. Basquiat always jumped from one painting to another, so he maintained his interest and energy. You have more strength and power than you appreciate – it would help if you devised ways of bringing it out of yourself.

2   Set a deadline. A deadline will force you to prioritize tasks and stop you from procrastinating. Don't think in terms of a nine to five day; there are twenty-four hours in a day. To meet the deadline for this book, I've been writing day and night for months, and if you have to work all night to meet your deadline, so what? I used to get illustration commissions and worked all night to complete them on time. It was nice working at three in the morning – I'd look out and see cars going by. Lock yourself in a room until you're finished. If you enjoy your work, you'll enjoy doing a lot of it.

3   Don't sacrifice quality. Work hard, but focus hard. There's no use producing lots of substandard work.

Are you crazy enough?

It was a pivotal moment in Wolfgang Pauli's career. If his scientific presentation on quantum physics went well, his career could take off; if it went badly, he'd disappear into obscurity. Pauli was worried about the reaction of the eminent scientists that filled the vast auditorium at Columbia University, because he knew his proposal would sound crazy.

After Pauli finished his presentation, Nobel Prize-winning physicist Niels Bohr gave his reaction, and it went down in history. He said to Pauli, 'We are all agreed that your theory is crazy. The question that divides us is whether it is crazy enough to have a chance of being correct.' It revealed Bohr's radical thinking. He wasn't looking for a good idea that made sense, he was only interested in a concept so new that it seemed crazy. Bohr was one of the most significant and revolutionary physicists of the twentieth century. He understood what lesser scientists didn't – a brilliant idea seems mad because it's counterintuitive and challenges the authority of established ideas. For Bohr, it wasn't enough for a concept to be crazy; it needed to be extremely crazy. Those at the top of science, business, or the arts are not afraid of ideas so new they seem ludicrous. It's why they're at the top.

A strange dance began. Pauli and Bohr paced around each other on the stage of the lecture theatre, arguing to and fro. Pauli explained why the theory was sufficiently crazy. Bohr stepped forward and clarified why it wasn't. The two giants of modern physics were arguing whether the idea was crazy enough – not whether it was logical, reasonable or coherent enough. Bohr felt the theory didn't have 'the divine madness of great physics'. The same is true of art, music, business or anything – a great idea has divine madness. At that level, all the scientists are incredibly intelligent; there is little to distinguish them. But Pauli and other scientists were satisfied with something crazy. This incident highlights the fact that although Bohr was one of many brilliant scientists, what made him exceptionally bright was his search for an extremely crazy idea.

1   Look at the work that's in front of you now and ask yourself, 'Would Bohr consider it crazy enough?' 'Does it have divine madness?'

2   Listen to sensible advice from sensible people and you'll produce something sensible. It's the crazy ones with mad ideas who push forward and transform the world. If people like your ideas, it's because they are reasonable and logical – that means you're doing something badly wrong. Your ideas must challenge people.

Build your wings as you fall

A paper aeroplane made from a fifty-franc note floated down a Parisian boulevard. An excited passer-by lunged for it, more notes followed, and a crowd scrambled for them. The source was artist Maurice de Vlaminck, who had sold a painting and gone on a three-day drinking session with his friend Modigliani. They bought expensive bottles of wine, made paper aeroplanes with banknotes, and threw them into the street. Vlaminck was soon broke. Reckless fool! Well, not really. Vlaminck realized he worked with more drive when he was desperate. When he was financially comfortable, he painted like a sloth. He earned vast sums of money, but it was spent or invested in accounts that he couldn't access. Plenty of cash made him lazy, and weak in ambition. His purpose was to produce brilliant work – and he realized he worked at maximum potential when he was on the brink.

Vlaminck went down in the history of art for creating the Fauves movement with Henri Matisse and Derain. Getting a project like his career or the Fauves off the ground required the same power as launching an aircraft. Imagine your life and career are an aircraft, and you are the pilot; you have to understand the forces working for and against you to be able to manage them.

Make yourself desperate. The artist Alex Katz explained, 'If you're going to go for "it", you have a common thing you share with other artists; that's desperation. You jump out a window style-wise. Try to put it together before you hit the ground.' The real creative person understands you can't build your wings and then fly; you have to be falling through the air. It is only desperation that will make you build wings that work. It's only that sinking feeling that will make you do great things – the sight of the ground rushing towards you. If you build your wings while standing firmly on the ground, you can procrastinate, make shoddy wings, and be unfocused. The steps you need to take only reveal themselves when you take action. For one thing, you'll eliminate all distractions.

My father was in the RAF (I was born in a house on an RAF housing quarter) and I used to stand with my father and watch fighter jets take off. He'd explain the four forces that apply to flight, thrust, drag, weight, and lift. Those forces can also lift our careers and lives and make them fly.

Thrust

An engine provides thrust and pushes your plane forward. If thrust is stronger than drag, your plane accelerates (Newton's second law). Vlaminck worked out what drove him and how to push himself forward. He needed to rise above the thousands of other artists working in his field. You need a passion for your work that will help you soar above the pressures of everyday life. What powers you? To rise above other artists, Vlaminck realized he had to shake off traditional art limitations and free himself from constraints. He was thrust forward by the desire to improve, expand and develop as a person. Consciously build your motivation. Our motivation is erratic; it comes and goes unpredictably, and disappears when we need it most. It would help if you worked on your motivation and built it up. Maintain your hunger. Find the subject you most care about to build deeper and dependable motivation. All successful people find ways to be highly motivated.

Drag

Drag opposes thrust. Put your hand out of a car window: the force of the wind pushing your hand back is 'drag'. The drag on our careers is often our fears and insecurities. Optimism must lift us over them. Safety makes us sluggish when we need

a state of heightened alertness. You'll only produce brilliant work if you overcome the drag from friends', family and colleagues' negativity.

A tightrope walker with a safety net falls off a lot more than one without one. Don't construct safety nets around yourself; Vlaminck deliberately destroyed safety nets because he knew the negative effect they'd have. To produce something great, every step forward has to be an adventure – a risk. What is producing drag in your career and life?

Weight

Weight opposes lift. If weight and lift are equal, a plane flies level at a constant speed. The more weight there is, the more lift is needed, so a massive aeroplane finds it harder to take off than a light aircraft. Aeroplanes are designed to be light, so develop yourself to be light. The past can drag us down. What weight can you lose? What unnecessary loads are you carrying? The pressures from school and family hold us down on the runway and prevent us from lifting off.

Lift

Lift can overcome weight. Because air moves faster above the wings of a plane than below, it creates lift. The wings push up because there's less force above them. If lift exceeds weight, then your aircraft can fly.

Vlaminck found ways to lift the pressure off himself. He lifted himself beyond everyday concerns and could see the art world hidden from above. Financial success made him complacent and heavy. You don't have to make paper aeroplanes with your money, but you do need to work out how to keep yourself or your organization light and sturdy. If you're hungry, your thinking will be alert.

When your project is finished, your work begins

There is a fable that haunts many writers. It's a lesson for novelists or anyone involved in a personal project, and the extraordinary tale reminds us that it's not enough to produce brilliant work. You have to be excellent at promotion.

Writing books was a matter of life and death to John. He considered he was destined to be a novelist and poured his heart into writing his book. John believed his novel was a million-selling, Pulitzer Prize winner. He submitted the manuscript to a publisher, but to his astonishment it was rejected. To him, the book was a masterpiece; how could they not see it? Publisher after publisher turned it down until there were none left to approach. He took radical, decisive action and tragically took his own life.

John's mother, Thelma, took up the torch for his book and tried several different publishers, unsuccessfully. Thelma turned her attention to other writers for help. She persistently called an author, Walker Percy, to enlist his support. He eventually relented: 'The lady was persistent, and it somehow came to pass that she stood in my office handing me the hefty manuscript. There was no getting out of it.' He continued, 'I read on . . . with a prickle of interest, then a growing excitement, and finally an incredulity: surely it was not possible that it was so good.' He helped her find a publisher. The book was an instant commercial and critical hit, did indeed win the Pulitzer Prize, and sold over a million copies.

The reason authors are obsessed with this story is because it's true. The author was John Kennedy Toole, and his book was entitled *A Confederacy of Dunces*. The tragedy was that Toole gave up too quickly. It's not the end of your role when you finish your book, painting or album. The problem was not the rejection but his attitude to it; he let the negativity of publishers crush him. I doubt if many publishers even read the manuscript because they often don't have the time. A writer's job is not just producing a book and standing back, it's promoting the book and arousing interest in the audience. Making it as brilliant as possible helps, of course – and you also have to make sure everyone knows about its brilliance. When you finish your project, it's not the end; it's the beginning of the end.

Toole is a warning not to give in to adversity. 'A problem is a chance for you to do your best,' said Duke Ellington. If ever you want to throw in the towel, think of Toole. Success might be just around the corner. You can manage your perception of rejection and use your intelligence to take creative action. Toole should have exploited the same creative thinking he'd used in his book to promote the novel.

You can't take your work too seriously – but you can take rejection too seriously. Stand up for your *Confederacy of Dunces*. Don't give up on it or let the negative opinions of others deflate you. Promote it by any means possible. If you're no good at promotion, get someone else to do it.

Your work should mean everything to you. Football manager Bill Shankly said, 'Football isn't a matter of life and death. It's more important than that.' The same is true of your work. Take what you do seriously, but never yourself.

1   Be as inventive with promoting your work as you are with producing it. It's human nature to think about the negative and forget all the positive actions we could take, so think about the practicalities of getting published, exhibiting in a gallery or signing a record deal. I've dedicated almost as much time to promoting this book as I did to writing it – making short films, rebooting my website, delivering podcasts, and everything else possible.

2   Find a professional to help you, like an agent or gallery curator. They have a deeper knowledge of the many routes into the business.

3   Avoid black and white thinking. There is never success or failure but a mixture of the two. Nothing is ever a dead end; there's always a way forward.

Action leads to enthusiasm, and then inspiration

What do you do when you are uninspired? If you sit and wait for the divine bolt of lightning to strike, you could be waiting forever.

I received a commission to deliver a talk on Michelangelo to a business audience of hundreds. I'd be flown halfway around the world, put up in a luxury hotel, and paid five figures for a thirty-minute talk. I felt under pressure to deliver something special. I knew there was a secret, something new and unexpected I could uncover about him, but what?

I used to hate public speaking because I'm shy. Yet I've given hundreds of talks as a university lecturer and public speaker, sometimes to over a thousand people. I discovered the only way to enjoy the experience was to believe in what I'm saying. To feel I am spreading useful knowledge that helps people.

Instead of waiting for inspiration, I knew I had to act. I went to see Michelangelo. I was in Florence when I received the commission, so I went to see Michelangelo's bust at the Casa Buonarroti. Daniele da Volterra created the sculpture after Michelangelo's death in 1564. Looking at his distinguished face, with its broken nose, I determined that my talk would leave an impression on the audience.

It's a myth that inspiration comes first for creative people, and that motivates them to act. The process is the exact opposite.

Tchaikovsky said, 'There is no doubt that even the greatest musical geniuses have sometimes worked without inspiration. This guest does not always respond to the first invitation. We must always work, and a self-respecting artist must not fold his hands on the pretext that he is not in the mood.'

If you act, you get lucky and stumble on things. If you wait until you feel inspired, you could be waiting for days or months without producing anything. An author with writer's block needs to start writing because you get ideas from doing something. A small action motivates you to take a further step and gives you a foundation to build on.

What could I say about Michelangelo that someone hadn't already said? I read books by academics who repeated information from other writers' books. For centuries, art historians portrayed him as the stereotypical misunderstood, struggling artist, and Michelangelo himself promoted himself as impoverished and exploited by his wealthy patrons. He wrote a poem about poverty and how he was 'poor, old, and working as a servant of others'.

In desperation, I even read the 500-year-old bank records of Michelangelo, which Professor Hatfield of Syracuse University discovered in Rome's city archives. They were extraordinary and blew away all the myths about him, which had sprung from academics focusing on his artworks and ignoring his finances. The bank records were as detailed as modern ones, with dates, amounts and names of who the money was received from, and paid out to. They showed that although Michelangelo grew up in poverty, he earned a fortune from his early twenties onwards, and quickly amassed enormous wealth. He was one of the wealthiest people on the planet.

Michelangelo never struggled financially. He was like a Premier League footballer showering property and jewellery on his family. He spent even more on wine than on marble. He invested wisely in property, such as a productive farm near Rome and mansions in central Rome and Florence. He left an estate worth roughly US$50 million in today's money. A stash of cash was found in a box under his bed when he died – 8,400 gold ducats, enough to buy a palace.

The theme for my talk was that great artists are as good at finance as they are at creativity. The public likes the idea that great artists don't care about money, but it's a narrative that prevents people from going into the arts. It's one of the lectures I'm most proud of and consider to have been genuinely revealing. I only showed images of his bank ledgers and none of his sculptures or paintings. It received a tremendous response and a standing ovation. (OK – I know it was really for Michelangelo and not for me.)

1 Don't fall into the trap of waiting to be inspired. Take action; search for something to spark your imagination. Cast your net wide because inspiration could be lurking in an unexpected place – like someone's bank accounts from hundreds of years ago.

2 Keep digging and researching until you find something that surprises you. If it amazes you, it will astonish others. If it isn't fascinating, why are you wasting people's time with it?

Become a fixer

We often forget to take the time to gain a deep insight into our field of work. Urgent but transient concerns cloud our minds, but we can't solve problems unless we get to the heart of things. A company in the business world, an artist in the art world, a scientist in a lab – whatever sphere you're working in, it's essential to understand the mechanisms of your field of activity. Then focus on making them work better: become a fixer.

In the 90s I visited one of the richest men in Britain, Paul Raymond. I was hesitant to meet him because he'd made his fortune from publishing porn magazines and running strip clubs and casinos. But he had been persuaded by his girlfriend to finance an art photography book that would not otherwise get funding.

The team, including my wife, worked on book layouts on a table in his Mayfair flat. The publication contained photographs that recorded the extraordinary characters in a club called Madame Jojo's in London's Soho. Owned and run by Raymond, Jojo's brought together a diverse nightlife of drag queens, the transgender community, and gay and burlesque culture.

Raymond, meanwhile, worked on his own at another table, fixing a faulty toaster. The toaster was cheap, hardly worth a few pounds, but he was trying to make it work. His partner was exasperated and kept imploring him to go and buy another one, and after the meeting, everyone talked about the meanness of someone so wealthy: not buying another but wasting hours trying to fix an old one.

The incident revealed the key to Raymond's thinking. He was drawn to things that weren't working to their full potential and he fixed them. He was the only person in the room not thinking about money – which was why he became the richest man in Britain. Everyone else thought buying a new toaster was the solution. Raymond was the only one focused on making the toaster work, and it was the key to his wealth. His first consideration wasn't money, it was getting things to work as efficiently as possible. He applied the same thinking to his magazines, nightclubs and casinos. He worked out how to make every aspect run more smoothly.

Most people think money is the solution to a problem, or they think about the costs, rather than fix what's wrong. Raymond spent hours fixing the toaster. It didn't make financial sense, but he was interested in making things work. Maybe you don't approve of casinos (though when we went to his casino, there were plenty of artists like Lucian Freud and Francis Bacon enjoying themselves), but for those who did, his casinos were the most pleasurable.

Raymond wasn't calculating about his time. Not because of kindness or helpfulness, but because it bugged him when something didn't work. One of my friends from art college became a film producer because he was a fixer. If a friend of his had a broken strap on their handbag, he'd fix it. If he saw a motorist broken down, he'd stop and spend hours trying to fix their car. He had a compulsion to fix things and wasn't confused by money like most of us – that's how he became successful, by adjusting one thing at a time. 'If we had been driven by money alone, we would have sold almost immediately,' said Larry Page, founder of Google. They received many acquisition offers when Google was a promising start-up. Page wasn't as interested in the potential millions as he was in helping people access information more easily.

How you deal with small problems is how you deal with huge issues. If you dedicate all your energy to fixing one small problem at a time, you'll find you produce something huge and worthwhile.

1   Adopt the fixer mentality and look for what isn't working. How does the field you work in function? How could it be better? Fixers look for things to fix, and it could be anything, anywhere. If you want to be wealthy, stop thinking about money and focus on what matters most to you.

2   Don't be influenced by other people's definitions of success. If you don't think of fame and riches as definitions of success, it frees you up to focus on what matters most to you. Define what success means – and it must be personal to you. Set about fixing anything that isn't working.

Which class of person are you?

Leonardo da Vinci said, 'There are three classes of people: those who see, those who see when they are shown, those who do not see.' Our task is to become 'those who see' and notice the possibilities around us. We are all born into the 'those who do not see' group but can elevate ourselves to the 'see when they are shown' group with education. We have our eyes open but our minds shut, and never 'see' what is around us. We must join 'those who see' and be alert and aware of the value (and I don't mean monetary value) of our surroundings.

We can look to two Austrian students, Sally Bibawy and Matthias Fiegl, for an insight into how to become 'those who see'. They discovered a 35mm LC-A Compact Automat Camera in a second-hand shop when visiting Prague in 1992. Soviet citizens hated the camera, manufactured by the Leningradskoje Optiko Mechanitscheskoje Objedinzinie factory, for four reasons:

* The design was unfashionably chunky and clumsy
* It was poorly assembled from cheap plastic and light leaked through the cracks causing streaks on the film
* The viewfinder didn't align with the lens, so when you took a photo, it didn't correspond with your selected view. If you photographed your friend, you ended up with a tree behind them. You couldn't be sure what would end up in the photo

* The lens had a strange coating that created extreme optical distortions. The colours were lurid and gaudy. It also made the photos out of focus, with a peculiar shadow around the edge of objects

When the USSR fell, imported goods, including Western cameras, flooded into Russia, and factories started to close as Western products became popular. In 1994 the Leningradskoje Optiko Mechanitscheskoje Objedinzinie factory decided to discontinue manufacturing the 35mm LC-A Compact Automat camera and lay off 150 workers.

However, when Bibawy and Fiegl discovered the camera and used it, they were astonished. They thought it was brilliant for four reasons:

* They loved the chunky, clumsy design because it was matter of fact and unpretentious. It wasn't smoothly contoured, overdesigned and covered in dials and buttons like Western cameras
* They loved how it was poorly assembled and let light in to create random streaks on the film
* They were excited at the way the viewfinder didn't align with the lens and the randomness that resulted. It added excitement – you never knew how your photo would turn out. There was no point in trying to compose a frame like fussy, professional photographers
* They loved the strange lens coating that made lurid colours, the peculiar shadow around objects, and the fact that the photos were out of focus. Brilliant! No point wasting time focusing!

The two Austrians saw something special in the camera, and showed it to their friends. Their enthusiasm was infectious, and a cult grew around the camera with hundreds, then thousands of followers. Their devotees couldn't pronounce Leningradskoje Optiko Mechanitscheskoje Objedinzinie, so they shortened it to LOMO, called their club the Lomographic Society International, and named themselves Lomographers.

The two Austrian Lomographers developed a philosophy – they encouraged lack of control and spontaneity, and embraced the unpredictable, intuitive and unexpected. 'Don't think, just shoot' became the Lomographers' motto. Devotees were encouraged, 'You can't plan anything! Don't think about it!' Take photos from odd angles, make strange compositions, and be uninhibited. They urged followers to 'eradicate all traces of your photographic education'. They showed how the best photos come from spontaneity and impulsiveness.

The Lomographers bought every LOMO they could get and resold them. They soon ran out, however, so they decided to buy directly from the factory. But it was due to close. Russians were buying Western cameras now that they had the opportunity, and the factory was going bankrupt. The two Austrian admirers asked to promote the camera in return for worldwide distribution rights. The factory signed an agreement with them thanks to a far-sighted, unknown bureaucrat (Vladimir Putin, later to become Russian president), in order to receive a tax break and keep the LOMO factory open, saving hundreds of jobs.

Lomography opened embassies – part shop, part gallery, part community headquarters – in Munich, New York, Paris, London and many other places around the globe. I used to drop into their LOMO Embassy in London. A sign there declared 'Don't Think, Just Shoot'. The walls and ceiling were papered from top to bottom with a patchwork of customers' photos. LOMO became the most fashionable camera in the world. Its success was down to the Austrians' genuine enthusiasm for a camera that brought spontaneity back to photography. Professional photographers had killed photography with their obsession with technical excellence.

The success of Lomography was to see the qualities others had missed. They didn't intend to build a successful business, but to share their vision. Most businesses fail because the entrepreneur is enthusiastic about making money rather than a view. Success is about seeing something unique and sharing your insight. Successful artists, entrepreneurs and scientists are often doing something disarmingly simple; they say, 'Look at this, it's amazing because . . .' Great artists, entrepreneurs and scientists have trained themselves to notice what we can't see, and they take time to communicate what they've seen. They help us to understand and make us feel that we have a unique vision and belong to their club.

Trusting to personal intuition has become a more everyday experience with the invention of the camera phone. Suppose you want a LOMO? No need. There's a LOMO app.

1   Nurture an open-minded attitude. Imagine yourself in the position of the two Austrians: if you'd found the LOMO, would you have recognized its qualities and communicated them? At the time, everyone wanted the most expensive, beautifully designed camera. Would you have had the mindset to disregard the fashion and want one with a faulty lens?

2   Look around. Develop the ability to truly 'see' and not wait for someone to show you. Give yourself the task of showing others, like the Lomographers did. It transforms you into an active person with a mission.

Construct > deconstruct > reconstruct

If you show your work and the response is 'It's good', the question you need to ask is 'How could I make it brilliant?'

Smash it up. Break it into pieces. Examine each element. Then put it back together differently. It's easier to examine and question each section when they've been separated. Take apart an object or organization and you can see right inside. Turn it upside down; this demystifies and clarifies. Deconstruction opens up possibilities and unleashes surprising options, so when you remake it, it's an opportunity to use and stretch your imagination. Try to put it back together in new, unexpected ways.

Cornelia Parker asked the British army to blow up an archetypal garden shed. After the explosion, the blackened pieces of wood and charred objects such as tools and flower pots were carefully gathered together. Parker suspended them from the ceiling as if in mid-explosion. A light in the centre of the fragments cast dramatic shadows on the walls. It was called *Cold Dark Matter: An Exploded View*. It was the same mundane garden shed, but by separating it into fragments, Parker forced you to see it in a completely new light. It's that new perspective we should all be searching for.

A deconstructivist architect takes a conventional building apart, then plays with putting the roof, floors, windows and doors back together in new and unexpected ways. The elements are put together so differently that the viewer is constantly surprised, and the building is liberated from the rules of architecture. Architect Rem Koolhaas and his studio OMA created a method that's anti-method: they take apart and question every accepted ready-made architectural practice each time they start a project. They systematically reject developing a systematic method.

Deconstruction breaks down a complex system into smaller systems so you can understand their role within the bigger system. This exciting method can be applied to anything – a painting, finance department, song, start-up business, car design . . . the possibilities are endless. Trying to understand the whole complex system can be overwhelming. Understanding is easier if you analyze each of the sub-systems, one by one, in isolation.

When I work as a creative consultant, whether in a hospital, bank or tech start-up, I often use diagrams as the first stage of problem-solving. I get those involved to lay out all the elements of the organization or product, usually on Post-it notes so they can be easily moved around. It's essential not to use any words, only images, even if it's just a scribbled drawing. It makes them quicker and easier to understand. Words slow the thought process down and add complexity. A complex system described with words is no help at all.

Suddenly everything is clear. We then experiment with reorganizing them. We can see each element of the organization separated, then we play with how we could put them back together differently. This is where we find all kinds of new ideas, and new possibilities emerge. Creating non-linear, visual diagrams is essential to working out these new, innovative directions.

1   Break your work into pieces. If you break your subject apart, it's easier to understand how all the elements fit together. I often take a photo of a large painting I'm working on, print out loads of copies, cut them up and remake it. It's easier to cut up copies and rearrange them than a huge painting.

2   Analyse each element in depth. Question how it has been put together. If you construct your work conventionally, you'll end up with a conventional construction. Deconstruction forces you to question and rethink everything about your project – especially your preconceived ideas. It reveals the underlying assumptions and frameworks in your field so you can break away from them.

3   Play with each element and invigorate your work by putting them back together in a new, unexpected way. If the elements are essential and can't be changed, they can at least be rearranged in a better way. For instance, doors, windows and staircases can't be removed from a building, but they can be moved around to make it more interesting as a whole.

A brilliant process creates brilliant work

I'm often asked by students and clients, 'How can I get ideas?' Here's my answer . . .

We are under pressure to produce results quickly. Deadlines loom, and we rush to get things finished. We don't have time to analyse how we work.

Instead of working on a project, work out how to work on a project. Design the steps you take. An exciting process leads to interesting ideas.

Jackson Pollock developed a unique process, and it led to exceptional work. There's a myth that Jackson Pollock discovered his 'drip' technique by accident, but it actually took him two decades. He began his career painting figures influenced by Native Americans. Year by year, the marks became more fluid and more abstract. Then bit by bit, he added dribbled lines until the pictures were entirely covered in drips.

The purpose of the creative process is to discover what we do best. Art critic Keith Sawyer wrote about Pollock, 'No great work ever emerges fully formed from the mind. People become known as "exceptional creators" not because of the power of their inspiration, but because of the intensity and dedication of their work process; because of their ability to stay focused through multiple revisions; and because of their ability to negotiate a zigzag path from the first glimmer of an idea to the final full-fledged work.'

Your process is how you will spend your time. If you don't enjoy the process, you won't enjoy your working life. Being experimental, exploring, and pushing into new areas keeps you alive and energized.

If you were commissioned to design a building to communicate 400 years of African American history and culture, how would you get ideas?

Architect David Adjaye won the competition to design the Smithsonian National Museum of African American History and Culture, and built one of America's most significant buildings. Adjaye spent eleven years travelling to all fifty-four countries in Africa and published the observations in a book, *African Metropolitan Architecture*. His extensive research gave him the first-hand experience he needed for the commission, and the Yoruban caryatid inspired the three tiers of the inverted pyramid he used for the museum. Every design decision sprang from his research into African American history.

Adjaye said, 'All of my projects are rooted in research.' He produced numerous early conceptual sketches, and putting ideas on paper started the storytelling process. The new Smithsonian leads you through the narrative of African American history as the building itself moves upward, slowly lifting you into the light. The building is not just a collection of objects; the visitor feels they are inside the story.

You need something extraordinary about your process to create outstanding work, and at the core of Adjaye's process is research. Extensive enquiry enables you to make new connections between diverse ideas and unusual materials; in Adjaye's case, it led to the decision to cover the museum's outside facade in a bronze-coated alloy, patterned latticework screen that refers to African American ironworkers' historical patterns from the South. It gives the museum a powerful presence, making it an iridescent, golden colour in the sunlight that becomes dark and brooding in the evening.

1   Analyse how you work and design your process to make it exciting and inspiring. Brilliant process = brilliant work. If the process is intelligent, it leads to brilliant work.

2   Design your process based on the way you enjoy working, and make sure every day is fun and lively. A good process will give you confidence that you can take on any project.

3   Don't adopt the standard practices of your field. Develop your unique process, and you will produce unique work. The best way to work is to first design how you work. Artists like Jackson Pollock develop a unique process of putting paint onto canvas, which leads to unique paintings.

Find the strongest move

As a university tutor, I don't want to always be delivering the same old lectures in the same old way.

I taught a film studies class for filmmaking students and my subject was an iconic film director. I wanted to teach them his six essential creative thinking methods, techniques useful for making the best decisions during any project, but also in life in general. I didn't want to follow the usual format, show clips of his movies and discuss them. His work was original and unique and I wanted to reflect his approach.

I put my students into groups of two and gave them a chess set from the chess club. They were irritated; they wanted to learn about film, not play games. I encouraged them to plan strategies and anticipate opponents' moves, and after some of the quickest, worst chess games in history, I explained that the film director Stanley Kubrick lived as a chess hustler before making films. He worked every day in Washington Square Park, earning money against chess players. His lifelong obsession with chess continued and he even played on film sets.

Kubrick made films like a chess player. In an interview with *Playboy* magazine, he compared chess to directing a film. On set, he exhausted all the possibilities (and the actors). He looked at every possible angle to shoot, and even when he had a good shot, continued to look for something better.

He was constantly rewriting the script and assessing all possibilities – even when under enormous financial pressure to finish the films. His background in chess made Kubrick a brilliant director.

He said, 'Among a great many other things that chess teaches you is to control the initial excitement you feel when you see something that looks good. It trains you to think before grabbing, and to think just as objectively when you're in trouble. When you're making a film you have to make the most of your decisions on the run, and there is a tendency to always shoot from the hip. It takes more discipline than you might imagine to think, even for thirty seconds, in the noisy, confusing, high-pressure atmosphere of a film set. But a few seconds' thought can often prevent a serious mistake being made about something that looks good at first glance.'

Whatever your project, don't jump for the first, obvious choice; consider the consequence of each move. Kubrick was a disciplined director because chess taught him strategy. Making a film is a battle against obstacles and problems, and achieving the best outcome is a slippery and unpredictable business.

One of the most common problems I deal with when working as a consultant for an organization is the client settling for the first idea – if it's OK. They're so relieved to solve the problem that they jump ahead, and I have to encourage them to continue to see if there is a better, brilliant solution. Find multiple solutions to any problem, then pick the best one. For each illustration I did for this book, I did five or six, then chose the strongest. Don't settle for a good enough answer; it has to be brilliant. The great artists, scientists and entrepreneurs are never satisfied with the first solution.

'The blunders are all there on the board, waiting to be made,' said chess grandmaster Savielly Tartakower. Blunders ruin your project. The great chess players attack to win, but most of their effort goes into avoiding errors. Rather than rush headstrong into an attacking move, they avoid a stupid one. 'One bad move nullifies forty good ones,' said chess master Israel Albert Horowitz. It's a great way of thinking about your work and life: whatever you're doing, it's important to make the best possible move. Kubrick annoyed his film crews by spending hours looking for the best shot.

He often shot the same scene repeatedly. In *The Shining*, there's a scene where Shelley Duvall waves a baseball bat at Jack Nicholson as he pursues her, which Kubrick filmed 127 times. In another scene, a character discusses the ability to 'shine' with a young boy. Kubrick took 148 takes to get it the way he wanted. Find the best move by considering all the possible alternatives, no matter what pressures are on you.

1   Seize the initiative. Chess players aim to control the board, and if you allow others to take command, you won't like the result.

2   The starting point usually determines the endpoint. Assess the situation at the outset, and only make a move if it's the best one possible.

3   A project and our life is a series of decisions, but we take many of these decisions without thinking deeply. A wrong choice can lead you into a maze. If a good opening appears, don't jump at it, look for a better option first. Don't make a move simply because you can or because you are impatient. Emanuel Lasker, a great chess player and philosopher, warned against beginners' chess: they see a good move, and their pent-up excitement gets the better of them. Lasker urged inexperienced players to search for alternatives and not worry about the time required. Kubrick never rushed into making a decision before considering every option.

4   Learning to work out what other people are thinking is crucial, because then you can predict their actions.

5   A chess player must focus for hours. One lapse of concentration, and they lose. And this is true with any project: an error in decision-making can be critical. Our culture trains us to flick channels, click social media likes and look for instant gratification. But the longer you concentrate, the better your work will be.

6   The best chess players attack. You can't win by defending. As Savielly Tartakower said, 'Nobody ever won a chess game by resigning.' Attack your project by throwing all your energy into making the best moves.

Back to my film class – for the rest of the term I started lessons with chess, and the students were enthusiastic because they appreciated how chess benefitted Kubrick. Some even joined the university chess club.

Be a big-picture thinker and a details thinker

Research by psychologists has proved there are two character types, a 'big picture thinker' or a 'detail thinker'. We are all one or the other, and we must work hard at developing the trait we lack. There are problems and blessings associated with each type, of course: the detail-oriented are meticulous and thorough but lose a sense of perspective; big-picture people are creative and visionary but overlook the minutiae.

It would be best if you were both, so identify which one you are and try to develop your other attribute. Cultivate the mindset you lack, and quickly switch between both.

The worst advice you could receive is 'be realistic'. We have aeroplanes because the Wright brothers were unrealistic, cars because Ford didn't listen to reason. If details start to drag down your project, switch to big-picture thinking. When you're lost in dreams, pull yourself back to earth by thinking about practical details.

Research shows three positive traits of big-picture thinkers:

* They are creative and full of inspiring ideas
* They are highly motivated because they don't brood over problems but invent new ideas for solutions
* They see patterns in problems because they view the overall picture and are not distracted by details

The negatives about big-picture thinkers are:

* They don't tolerate repetitive tasks and either completely overlook or are sloppy about details

The positives about detail thinkers are:

* They are organized, precise and analytical
* They are efficient and they make sure work is completed
* They are good at improving something that already exists (rather than creating something new)
* They have high standards and produce work of the highest quality

The negatives about detail thinkers are:

* They overthink the details and can't see the big picture. They lack perspective and fail to prioritize

Any project requires both modes of thinking. A film director must keep in mind the plot (big picture) while filming each shot (the details). When filming *Reservoir Dogs*, Quentin Tarantino focused on each small detail of the set in front of him but kept in mind how it related to the overall concept. He luxuriated in the fine details of the dialogue. His characters bicker about the ethics of tipping waiters and the meaning of a Madonna song, but the conversations help you understand the characters' role in the overall plot – a jewellery heist goes wrong, and the surviving criminals suspect one of them is a police informant.

Be the director of your work. Train your mind to deal with small issues and simultaneously keep the bigger goal in mind.

Details can be a forest that you become lost inside. Find your way through the undergrowth while simultaneously observing from a bird's-eye view.

Negative experience = positive result

We all suffer crises and bad experiences, the destruction of something precious, humiliation, or maybe you're stuck in a boring place.

The people you admire, those who achieve great things, found a way to use it in their work when they were in an uninspiring place or something terrible happened to them. If you're a creative person, everything is fuel; everything is a useable building material.

Andy Warhol's life changed when he bought a tape recorder. He said, 'Nothing was ever a problem again, because a problem just meant a good tape, and when a problem transforms itself into a good tape, it's not a problem anymore.' When he started keeping a diary, it turned a bad experience into a good diary entry. Whether mugged in the street, insulted by a cab driver or snubbed by a celebrity, it made him happy because he had something dramatic to put in his diary. Everything is useful if you search for a way of finding the positive in it. The creative have a way of making a fortune out of misfortune.

Years ago, some passengers sat in the airport moaning about their fate. A flight leaving Puerto Rico for British Virgin Islands was cancelled. An airport lounge is a boring place if you aren't flying anywhere. One of the passengers had an idea. Many planes were sitting outside the terminal, and he wondered about chartering one. It was possible, but too expensive. But he calculated that if every delayed passenger paid him US$39, it would be affordable. He found a chalkboard, put the proposal to the passengers, and they all signed up.

As a joke, he wrote 'Virgin Airlines' at the top of the chalkboard. He ran a music company called Virgin Records and was, of course, the entrepreneur Richard Branson. He explained, 'I hired a plane and borrowed a blackboard, and as a joke I wrote Virgin Airlines on the top of the blackboard, US$39 one way to BVI. I went out round all the passengers who had been bumped and I filled up my first plane.'

After the flight, a passenger joked that Virgin Airlines was pretty good, and the comment sparked an idea. Back in England, Branson phoned Boeing and asked to buy a second-hand 747. They requested the name of his company, and he answered, 'Virgin.' Advisors told him no one would ever fly with an airline called 'Virgin'. The airline wasn't Branson's big expansion plan or strategic company development, but his humour, optimism and audacity transformed a bad experience into a positive result.

Writer Jorge Luis Borges explained the mindset of the creative person faced with a crisis: 'A writer – and, I believe, generally all persons – must think that whatever happens to them is a resource. All that happens to us, including our humiliations, our misfortunes, our embarrassments, all is given to us as raw material, as clay, so that we may shape our art.' A writer stuck at the airport would write about the passengers' reactions (Arthur Hailey wrote *Airport* about an airport struck by a storm). A musician would find inspiration for a song (John Denver wrote 'Leaving on a Jet Plane' while stuck at Washington Airport). An artist would make a sculpture based on their observations (Sacramento Airport features sculptures of giant towers of baggage, entitled *Samson* by Brian Goggin).

Like many of us, a schoolboy had a miserable time at school. They didn't take his favourite subject, art, seriously. He hated school because he went up and down the central staircase so often every day, it seemed infinite. It represented putting lots of effort into achieving nothing.

The schoolboy was M. C. Escher, and after he left school, he drew visual conundrums of the staircase. People walked upstairs but were simultaneously walking down. 'Only those who attempt the absurd will achieve the impossible. I think it's in my basement . . . let me go upstairs and check,' he said. Escher explored eternity and the impossible in realistic prints that are popular because people can relate to the feeling of going nowhere. His most miserable experience inspired his life's work.

1   What can you use from a bad experience? A crisis is an opportunity if you decide to use it. Most people see bad experiences as bad experiences, but the creative see them as useful, something of substance. Personal misfortune is something we all experience, so use it. Don't indulge in self-pity or complain about fate – act.

2   The creative learn how to get the maximum potential out of their experiences, and bad experiences are often a more abundant source of inspiration than gratifying situations. They help you to understand the strengths and weaknesses of your mind.

An idea is an engine

Projects kick off full of energy but often run out of steam. An idea holds your work together and keeps it driving forwards; it's an engine to power your way through the inevitable problems you'll encounter. An idea acts as a beacon to light the way and guide you. When there are economic pressures, severe problems or a client has doubts, a strong concept strengthens your conviction.

Architects usually design buildings, but architect James Law created a planet – a big, inspiring construction in Mumbai nicknamed 'The Egg'. It's a building with a self-contained, sustainable, natural ecosystem like a planet, where high levels of natural light create low-energy demand, while solar-energy panels and wind turbines generate electricity. There's a rainwater recovery system and water recycling process, and a garden that provides a quiet sanctuary and oxygen to cool the atmosphere. It's a self-contained mini world delivering an enjoyable environment in which to live and work. The latest

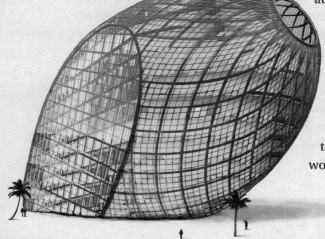

technology enables The Egg to be aware of the heating and lighting and adapt it as necessary – it's a 'smart' building, a conscious entity. It looks like a small planet that's crashed into the earth and it's the embodiment of the open-minded, creative thinking sweeping through India. It's a building you can fall in love with, feel a deep emotional attachment to, because it's more than just a structure – it's an idea.

The Egg is a gauntlet thrown down to other architects; can you provide something this good? Art, books, businesses, music and organizations improve society by adding new ideas and directions. Whoever you are and whatever your field, provide leadership by showing how things could be better.

Many people start a project with lazy thinking. You need to be totally focused from the outset. If you start in a sloppy way, the sloppiness will continue; before you start a project, sum it up in one sentence. Once you are clear what the central idea is, other decisions fall into place. The Egg was an office block, but an office block with a difference: they knew what they were intending to achieve. This first sentence, this first idea is key. Don't progress until you've it sorted out. The sentence enables you to ask, is it worth doing, is it a compelling idea?

During a talk I gave at Tate Modern, London, someone in the audience asked, 'Can you think of an example of a great idea?' Two artworks came to mind. The first was a famous poster created in 1989 by the Guerrilla Girls. A female nude from a classical painting lay next to the slogan 'Do women have to be naked to get into the Met Museum?' It highlighted the fact that only 15 per cent of the artists shown in the Metropolitan Museum in New York were women, but 85 per cent of the nudes were female. The art collective fought sexism in the art world, and it was a powerful idea: once seen, you can't forget it. They had a core idea and everything they did related to it.

The other work I used to demonstrate the power of an idea to leave a lasting impression was Salvador Dalí's *The Persistence of Memory*. In this painting, often more casually entitled *Soft Clocks*, Dalí illustrates melting watches to show how arbitrary and erratic our concept of time is. When we're bored, it goes slowly; when we're excited, it goes fast. Dalí's melting clocks symbolize Albert Einstein's theory of relativity. He proposed a new concept of time as being relative, not something fixed and easily tracked with a watch. The soft watches lose their certainty; they are not persistent. Once seen, it's an unforgettable image.

Ideas are what make human beings unique in the animal kingdom – they're the most incredible thing we produce. If you don't have ideas, you're not making use of your most valuable asset. A concept can make a building – or anything – stimulating, funny, adorable or entertaining. The great designer Karl Lagerfeld said, 'I am up to 90 per cent virtual.' He meant he was more of a concept than he was flesh and blood. He had a clear idea of himself, what he stood for and what he was trying to achieve. It made the brands he worked for understand what he was about and what he was aiming at. Ideas are democratic and can come from anyone, with any background, anywhere.

A momentous event took place in 1992: Microsoft's valuation overtook that of General Motors. It seemed that from then on, economies would be service-led, not manufacturing-led. In manufacturing, the value of a company lies in its machinery and property, but in a service company, like Microsoft, its value is in its ideas. That means investing in concepts and upgrading them rather than investing in better machinery. It's imagination that powers modern business; as Joseph Stalin said, 'Ideas are more powerful than guns.' People fall in love with an idea in the same way they fall in love with a person and feel the same loyalty and commitment.

1   Make your idea inspiring. The Egg is a planet that's good for the planet. People are drawn to ideas that are uplifting and stimulating. Start a song, novel, business or artwork with a big, powerful idea. Build a planet, not an office block. Don't move forward until you're sure your concept is great.

2   Become an ideas person. The more you have, the more easily you have them. My book *Ideas Are Your Only Currency* contains exercises I set my Central Saint Martins students. They transform people into idea generators. I want my students to be ideas people and come up with multiple concepts, quickly. I don't want them to think of themselves as a fashion designer, a sculptor or a graphic designer, but an ideas person. Coming up with ideas is rewarding, frustrating and exasperating, but it is where your true self emerges. As photographer Richard Avedon said, 'Start with a style, and you are in chains; start with an idea, and you are free.'

Four ways to overcome creative block

Hergé, the creator of the Tintin books, described his nightmare to the psychiatrist Franz Riklin: 'In an immaculately white alcove, a white skeleton appeared that tried to catch me. And then instantly everything around me became white.' Hergé suffered from a creative block and developed a horror of the white page. His dreams were of white doors, white snow, white walls, white everything. The psychiatrist advised him to kill off Tintin and retire, because work was destroying his mental health.

Hergé ignored the psychiatrist's advice. He studied his creative block and found five ways to rescue himself. Luckily, they're useful to us all.

Creativity sometimes asks us to dig deep and fight. If you fail, you can reassure yourself that you did everything possible, and you can be at peace with yourself. But if you don't try with all your might, you'll always feel you let yourself down.

Tintin had become an enormous industry, run from a large studio with many illustrators working on books, magazines, newspaper supplements and merchandising. The pressure to produce plotlines for books, draw them, colour them and run a team was enormous. Many people relied on Hergé for their livelihoods, and thousands of readers waited weekly for the next instalment.

Hergé had poured all his ideas into Tintin and felt empty. He began to see Tintin as a tyrant dictating his life. As well as suffering from nightmares, Hergé developed psoriasis of the hands and found it painful to pick up a pencil. His body was trying to prevent him from working. The romantic poets assumed writer's block was due to a higher power that wanted to stop them writing. They were right, but that higher power was their subconscious. Almost every creative person has struggled with being blocked, from author F. Scott Fitzgerald to composer Sergei Rachmaninov to songwriter Adele. Hergé knew that to give up, as the psychiatrist urged, was not the answer. Creativity was not the problem but the solution. When a creative person is lost, they have to be their own search and rescue team. When everyone urges you to take a break, go on holiday with them, go for a drink, or go to the beach, you must continue to work out your problem.

Hergé found his solutions. He visited the psychiatrist Riklin once and never returned. He instinctively knew that creativity was the answer, and his solution was to focus on the subject that mattered most to him. His mind was preoccupied with writer's block, so he wrote about his struggles with the blank page. He drew Tintin roaming around on white sheets, lost in blankness. A story emerged: Tintin trudging across vast expanses of snow in the Himalayas, searching and searching – just like Hergé.

The story of *Tintin in Tibet* is Tintin's search for his friend Chang Chong-Chen. In the book, the authorities declare that Chang has died in a plane crash in the Himalayas, but convinced that Chang has survived, Tintin sets off with Snowy to find him. They are overwhelmed by an avalanche of pure white snow but trek onwards, unable to lie down and sleep in case they freeze.

Tintin in Tibet was unusually philosophical for a comic book of the time and explored extrasensory perception, friendship and the mysticism of Tibetan Buddhism. It is existentialist like a Samuel Beckett play, and nothing happens other than Tintin's search for his friend; its very emptiness confused the publisher. Hergé's original front cover showed Tintin and his expedition against a white background, but the publisher was horrified and insisted Hergé add a mountain and many other features.

Hergé considered it his masterpiece, and the critics and public agreed. It was translated into thirty-two languages, made the subject of many museum exhibitions and adapted for television, radio, documentary, theatre and a video game.

Hergé used the book as a device to overcome traumatic nightmares and inner conflict. The answer to the creative block is to work out what you want to say. If it's difficult or even painful, it doesn't mean it's going wrong; it's just hard. Hergé understood salvation lies in creativity, confronting your problems, and using art to find a solution. Artist Philip Guston said, 'I go to my studio every day because one day I may go and the Angel will be there. What if I don't go and the Angel came?'

When you're creatively blocked, try these ideas:

* Your starting point should always be your primary interest. Ask yourself what matters most to you, find images and phrases to do with your theme and then put them up on a wall to analyse and discuss them.
* It's always the right time. You don't have to be in the right mood or the right frame of mind, it's still a good time to

write, paint or compose. Hergé was in a bad situation but he used his work to rescue himself.

* Don't give in to fear, embrace it. Creative people struggle with anxiety because they reveal their inner thoughts for everyone to see and judge.

* Start a massive project with small, modest steps. In George Orwell's novel *Keep the Aspidistra Flying*, the character Gordon Comstock struggles to complete an epic poem. 'It was too big for him . . . it had simply fallen apart into a series of fragments.' A solution I use in my workshops is to break a task into small, manageable jobs then slowly piece them together.

Disrupt or be disrupted

The speed of change makes nonsense of strategic planning. Sudden developments in technology create uncertainty, causing anxiety; unexpected events disrupt your routines, and confusing new ideas appear almost daily. But there is a way of dealing with and prospering from the chaos . . .

It was a typical early-morning rush hour at London's Liverpool Street Station in 2009. The commuters hardly glanced at the posters and billboards as they passed with blank, fixed expressions. They milled about like sleepwalkers, their only concern to get from A to B. The usual announcements blared out over the loudspeakers. Suddenly, lively dance music boomed out and a hundred commuters broke into a choreographed but unannounced song and dance routine. The dancers were not dressed as dancers but as ordinary commuters. Other commuters were stunned; they froze and watched. Passers-by were unsure how to react, then they were excited, they laughed, they reached for their phones, and they shared photos of the event. It was one of the first-ever flash mobs.

The event was created by ad agency Saatchi & Saatchi for T-Mobile's 'Life's for Sharing' campaign. Hidden cameras in the station captured the commuters' excited reaction. Footage was edited and aired on social media, went viral, and was shared by millions. Bam! Social media marketing was born. T-Mobile used the public's phones to promote their brand.

It won best TV commercial of the year award. The campaign was cheap to make and attracted millions of viewers, and it disrupted traditional advertising by turning the usual processes upside down.

When I act as a creativity consultant to businesses, I'm astonished at how most entrepreneurs and CEOs tell me they don't just want a successful business (as if that wasn't hard enough) but also to change the way the system works. They want to disrupt the luxury goods market, pharmaceutical market, eyewear market, etc. The overused term 'disruption' is not about causing chaos, it's about creating something so different that it destroys old methods. Artists have always wanted to disrupt the art world, from Manet to Banksy. Manet arranged group exhibitions to compete with the all-powerful salon; Banksy ignored the gallery system, published a book of photos of his graffiti and reached the public directly. They didn't just break the rules, they rewrote them.

But how do you disrupt the system? Saatchi & Saatchi noticed a few amateurish, poorly organized flash mobs, but they saw the untapped potential in a new media. You need to set up your own radar system and pick up new ideas in their infancy. Then develop them fully and you'll be at the forefront.

Famous individuals and organizations are less agile and are slow to adapt to new methods, so look at your field in a way established organizations are unable to. Elon Musk's company Tesla turned convention on its head. They had their antennae up, picked up new ideas, and exploited them. To protect innovation, usually technology companies patent it immediately, but Musk made his company, SpaceX, patent-free, and explained, 'We essentially have no patents at SpaceX

. . . If we published patents, it would be farcical because the Chinese would just use them as a recipe book.' Musk disrupted how we conduct money transactions with PayPal, use energy with Tesla, and space travel with SpaceX.

Disruption is going to happen to you, so your approach has to be so new it disrupts your field. Change is the new status quo. So, disrupt or be disrupted.

1   Set up a radar system to detect the latest ideas the moment they happen. They will disrupt your field of work simply by being new.

2   Find ways to go around the obstacles the system puts in your way. Gain a deep understanding of the system, find a gap, and work within that opening. Disruptors change things for the better, not for the sake of it. If the system is holding them back, they change it.

3   Put innovation before 'best practice'. Organizations believe in sharing best practice, but repeating what everyone is doing doesn't break new ground. Code and Theory is a creative company singled out by Nasdaq as a business disruptor. Because they believe 'best practices' can be obstructive, they encourage employees to focus on new methods, have the freedom to try out new ideas, and ignore the old ones. It's an inspiring attitude.

Being the best you

We're so busy working for more recognition, promotions or a higher income, we often lose sight of the more profound, more meaningful objectives we want to achieve.

A clear idea of your ideal lifestyle gives you a sense of purpose and direction when unexpected events try to knock you off course. Set your objective, then regularly weigh up and assess whether you are on the right path.

Architect Frank Gehry played around with cardboard. He used it to build models of his buildings and found it a fascinating substance: cheap, eco-friendly, and satisfying to touch. Gehry glued many layers of robust and lightweight cardboard together to create the springy yet surprisingly strong Wiggle Chair in 1972. It sold thousands, and he shot to international stardom as a furniture designer. But he wanted to be an architect. A reputation as a furniture designer would interfere with the design world's perception of him – furniture designers rarely get commissions to design buildings, after all. Gehry spent weeks in deep thought. Eventually, he decided to withdraw the Wiggle Chair after only three months and turn his back on a fortune. It required a huge amount of courage to withdraw the chair and annoy the manufacturer and the retailers. But he had a clear vision of who and what he wanted to be. In 1990 when he had built a reputation as an architect, he reissued the Wiggle Chair and, once again, it was an instant bestseller. He went on to build a reputation as one of the world's most respected architects by designing the Guggenheim Museum in Bilbao and the Walt Disney Concert Hall in Los Angeles. He had a clear view of what he wanted to become – an architect – and nothing knocked him off course, not even success.

Organizations and companies need a clear idea of what they want to become. Microsoft's vision was to 'empower people with great software anytime, anyplace, on any device'; eBay's was to 'provide global trading for anyone to sell anything, anywhere'; and Nike's to 'make sport a daily habit'. Successful designers and artists know this too, of course: Max Ernst's purpose was to 'free myself from reason', while William Turner's ambition was to capture the fluctuating light, atmosphere, mists, vapours and sea-spray in nature. A clear mission is like a rudder on a ship; it keeps your thinking on course through storms and dangerous currents.

An American folk singer and songwriter had a clear vision of what he wanted to become: the voice of the oppressed. Instead of just writing songs that were popular, he wanted to use them to document the lives of the underclass of American society. Woody Guthrie recorded the injustices suffered by the oppressed and it gave his work power and purpose; but more importantly, everything he did led to his overall goal.

The self-discipline to resist temptation and stay focused on your long-term objective is critical. I've had numerous friends who've taken a job that didn't suit them because the money was good. Ten years later, they're stuck in the trap, unable to free themselves and become what they most wanted to be. Make sure your short-term goals are in tune with your long-term goal and that your ultimate goal is true to your core values.

1　　Develop a clear vision of who you want to become. Without visualizing who you want to be, you'll easily be distracted by random events. Rapper Jay-Z said, 'I couldn't even think about wanting to be something else; I wouldn't let myself visualize another life.'

2　　Visualize the steps you need to take to reach your destination. Keep one eye on your small steps and the other on your long-term goal. Develop a strong sense of where you're going and what you want to achieve – then carve your path through thick and thin.

3　　Don't let anything distract you from your vision. It's important to ask yourself, is this consistent with my authentic goals? Will this make me the best I can be? Is this a step forward to the person I most want to become?

Boost your creative confidence

A TV news camera captured the moment two huge curtains drew back to reveal a gigantic Picasso mural, *The Fall of Icarus*, in the UNESCO headquarters, Paris. A vast audience of royalty, celebrities, dignitaries and journalists witnessed the historical event, which was comparable to the unveiling of Michelangelo's altarpiece for the Sistine Chapel, the first performance of Beethoven's 5th Symphony, or the debut of Shakespeare's *Hamlet*. In 1958 Picasso was at the height of his fame and internationally recognized as a great artist, part rock star, and part historical figure.

Before the unveiling, Picasso smiled, bullish and confident amid the enormous, admiring crowd. He exuded self-assurance. He never hesitated in interviews, never said 'Um' or paused, but fired answers back like bullets. His movements were quick, precise, and his piercing black eyes fixed the interviewer with a steely gaze.

At the UNESCO headquarters, the gasps died down, and there was a stunned silence. The disjointed painting depicted people on a beach with a falling figure, but the audience was shocked because *The Fall of Icarus* was dreadful. Embarrassment swept through the crowd. Picasso sensed the change in mood and looked uncomfortable. The president of UNESCO was so angry, he cut short his scheduled speech.

No one was more stunned than Picasso, who assumed it was a masterpiece. Critics reasoned Picasso hadn't taken the commission seriously and had produced it too quickly. Picasso feared the damage to his reputation and led the critics to his studio where he showed tens of rough sketches that had taken him weeks and months, and small paintings exploring the figures and composition. They weren't convinced.

Maybe you're thinking they didn't appreciate modern art. Well, no. The critics were right. It was rubbish then, and it's rubbish now. I was lucky enough to see the painting for myself (it's still at UNESCO) and it lived up to its reputation, it was a confused mess. But a vast Picasso, worth millions, couldn't be removed.

Picasso went back with his friends in the evening to view the mural under floodlights. He decided not to sign it, as a way of saying, 'It's nothing to do with me!' He was asked to repaint it but replied, 'Why? I knew what I was doing!' Picasso would never go back, only forwards.

Although Picasso outwardly appeared self-assured, he struggled with a lack of confidence, just like all of us. He was deeply unnerved by the incident, and we know from his friends' diaries that he fell into a deep depression. The problem was not that everyone thought the mural was weak, but that Picasso thought it was brilliant. He began to doubt his judgment. For a creative person, trusting your intuition is vital.

If even Picasso could suffer from a lack of confidence, it could happen to anyone. How you manage the loss of faith is the key, and Picasso used two techniques to rebuild his self-assurance.

Creative courage is not something you're born with but something you have to nurture, and Picasso shows us confidence is a useful tool you have to protect. Picasso faced criticism his whole life, and one of his techniques to build his confidence was to actively do something. After each of his failures in self-belief, he immediately set to work producing small-scale sketches and paintings, building up to more substantial works slowly. Sitting around and thinking about your confidence undermines your self-belief.

Picasso's second technique was to rigorously assess what had gone wrong. He was able to take a hard look at himself and evaluate his mistakes. Self-awareness is essential. Picasso was desperate for approval and aggressively ambitious, but he did whatever it took to improve, which meant learning from failures.

It is a comfort to find that all great creative people are involved in a constant struggle with anxiety. 'A painter paints a picture with the same feeling as that with which a criminal commits a crime,' said Edgar Degas. If you break new ground and produce new ideas, critics will doubt you.

1   Taking action is a cure to lack of confidence. Japanese psychiatrist Dr Shōma Morita created Morita Therapy for mental health. Instead of wrestling and worrying about their neuroses, patients should act and do whatever is needed. We should work on a problem so intensively that there's no time for worry.

2   Confidence is something you have to nurture as if it were a plant. Feed it and protect it from extremes.

Escape the mediocrity trap

If your work is mediocre, it's because you stopped when it was good enough. You failed it. You didn't take it all the way and make it brilliant. Every project – a painting, novel, start-up business or album – seems mediocre at the halfway stage; it's down to you to haul it to the summit. The word 'mediocre' combines the Latin words 'medius', meaning 'middle', and 'ocris', meaning 'jagged mountain', so it means something like 'stopping halfway up a harsh mountain', or abandoning a difficult task halfway through.

It's natural to become discouraged halfway through any endeavour. The initial excitement dies down, the end seems a long way off, and all you can see are the problems ahead. Ever done any DIY? You think you can paint a wall in an hour or two, but then you realize you haven't factored in stripping the wallpaper. Then you discover the plaster is blown and will come off when you do so. Then that the mortar between the bricks is crumbling. Suddenly you're standing knee-deep in the rubble with no end in sight.

Most painters find a new subject for each painting. Even portrait painters paint different people. So the small 10-by-8-inch pictures of Peter Dreher were a revelation when I came across them in the Punta della Dogana in Venice. The realistic paintings of a straightforward, cylindrical glass of water placed centrally against a white wall differ slightly with a change in lighting and background, but Dreher has painted the glass

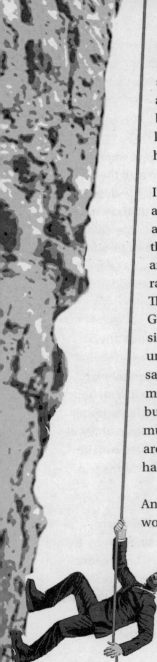

over 5,000 times, each time as if he'd never seen it before. He's kept up the intensity since 1974. Some reviews of Dreher's work are eulogizing, and others rip into them, but they are never neutral; people either love Dreher's persistence, and by extension his work, or they hate it.

I've met many of the world's great artists and musicians through my work at Central Saint Martins. When I talk to them about their work, you sense they are not interested in the end product, but rather how they made it – the process. They pursue brilliant ideas relentlessly. Governments, education and society sink towards mediocrity because the unexceptional is safe, but as Marlon Brando said, 'Never surrender to the momentum of mediocrity'. Brilliant work is transformative, but organizations fear transformation. You must create an anti-mediocrity culture around yourself, or people will hold you back halfway up a mountain.

Anything worthwhile is going to be hard work, so to succeed, you have to persist through the awkward middle stage. Novelist Thomas Mann said, 'A writer is someone for whom writing is more difficult than it is for other people,' by which he meant, writers embrace the difficulties. Overcoming the challenges is the rewarding part. New writers don't expect writing to be so torturous, and it doesn't become more comfortable with training or practice. This is true of any creative endeavour. Thomas Mann noticed that successful authors write slower than most people – indeed it seems that the more respected the writer, the slower they write. James Joyce took seven years to finish *Ulysses*, one of the greatest novels of all time, wringing out a hundred words a day. The great poet T. S. Eliot wrote six pages a year, a total of a hundred and fifty pages in his twenty-five-year career. Writing requires equal measures of self-discipline and inspiration.

The mountain is there for a purpose. It's there so you have an opportunity to show how badly you want to get to the summit. The reason it's jagged and doesn't have an elevator to the top is to show you what you must overcome. The daunting journey filters out the people who don't want it badly enough, but three techniques will ensure you climb the jagged mountain to the peak and reach 'brilliant':

1   Don't set off to climb a mountain until you are sure you believe in the task enough to see it through. Be entirely convinced you're doing the right thing, or you'll waver at the halfway stage.

2   Self-doubt always creeps in at the halfway point – it's natural. Don't find excuses to give up; it's just your subconscious justifying mediocrity. Instead, find reasons to continue. Remind yourself of your fundamental values. Many brilliant artists and entrepreneurs have a breakthrough idea. But the system they work in forces them to adopt its standard methods. They slowly find themselves doing what everyone else in the structure is doing. Be aware of how the system drags you back down to base camp. Halfway through this book, there was a point where the road ahead looked long – tens of chapters to rewrite, tens of illustrations to produce; like everyone, at the halfway point, I wondered whether it was all worthwhile.

3   Don't listen to negative voices. Once you've set out to produce something brilliant, you'll annoy others because you've highlighted how they've settled for mediocrity. Don't worry about producing exceptional work because of the criticism you'll encounter. You're inevitably doing what others aren't prepared to if you have higher aspirations. That will annoy them. John Steinbeck said, 'Only mediocrity escapes criticism.' Don't fear being ridiculed – fear mediocrity.

Control your ego, or it'll control you

Pride and a sense of self-importance drive us to produce something brilliant. Your ego is your core and what makes you different, so it must be protected and developed. We all need drive and ambition to make a success of demanding projects; your ego promotes you, and it drives you to prosper in a competitive workplace. But don't inflate it so much that it gets in your way.

We live in a social media culture that encourages us to pump up our ego and give in to our selfish impulses, but ego can also blind us to our faults, alienate us and lead to our downfall. It can prevent us from taking a hard look at ourselves, assessing what we're getting wrong, and doing whatever is necessary to put it right. Self-importance and arrogance can mess up your project because it distorts your understanding of what is going on. If we only care about getting what we want, we don't take advice or listen to feedback.

It's possible to train your ego to help and not hinder you, and it helps if you can manage, not suppress it. Be aware of how your ego can stir up your emotions and drive you to make the wrong decisions. If you can balance self-esteem with humility, you'll have the perfect launchpad for brilliant work.

Francis Ford Coppola was on a streak of success, collecting five Oscars for his work on *The Godfather* parts I and II. For an actor, a Coppola film meant a good chance of being nominated for, even winning awards. But when Coppola launched his new film project, every actor turned him down. He spent six years and millions of dollars in development, writing scripts, sending people to the Philippines to scout sites, raising the funding, and much more. He found it hard to sign up actors and film crew because no one wanted to spend months in the Philippines' humidity and rainy season.

When filming eventually started, actor Dennis Hopper was stoned and difficult. Coppola let him ramble as it fitted in with the psychedelic nature of the film. Coppola had paid Marlon Brando millions to take the role of charismatic, lean and self-disciplined Colonel Kurtz. When Brando appeared, he was several stone overweight and had shaved his head. He looked wrong for the part. And to make matters worse, Brando hadn't memorized his script or done any preparation.

Coppola found a way to coax a performance out of Brando by dressing him in black pyjamas and hiding him in shadows. Coppola here proves that a great film director rides the blows to their ego to protect their project.

In the jungle, everyone was irritable and tired because of the heat and humidity. Members of the production crew were affected by parasites and tropical diseases; one even died from rabies.

Coppola described an incident when he was sitting in a toilet cubicle in the men's room, and two crew members walked in chatting. One said to the other that the film was 'a load of shit, and the asshole director doesn't know what he's doing'. Coppola felt wounded by the comments, but he couldn't afford to take them personally. He batted them away for the sake of the project because he relied on the film crew to make a great film.

After a series of misfortunes, *Apocalypse Now* was released to massive critical and box office success. The chaos and confusion of the shooting helped capture the spirit of its subject – the Vietnam War.

1 Develop the ability to manage your ego and emotions. Understanding your feelings and how your moods affect others is critical. Subordinate your ego for the sake of your work; your project must have its own, separate ego.

2 Set out with the highest ambitions – but for the project, not for yourself.

3 Be the servant of your project. Artists, filmmakers and business people need drive and ambition to make a success of demanding tasks, but must put their ego to the side at times and do whatever is best for the project.

Design your life

Sometimes we feel our career or life has got out of control, gone up a blind alley or hit a roadblock. We know what our goals are but can't fulfil them.

Use a process called Design Thinking to design your life. Designers and artists use this five-step method to produce brilliant work, and it is the reason for the success of the iPhone, Tesla car, Anglepoise lamp and other excellent designs surrounding you. I've been teaching Design Thinking at art college, but also in banks, hospitals, pharmaceutical companies and technology businesses, because they realize the usefulness of creative thinking.

Apply Design Thinking to your life and become the architect of whoever you are and whatever you do, whatever your age.

Artist Henri Matisse composed his life in the same way as he did a painting or an exhibition. The method ensured he went from one brilliant career phase to another, decade after decade.

1 Understand yourself

There's no point embarking on a project until you understand yourself. Matisse dug deep into himself. What do you want to achieve? What are your strengths and weaknesses?

Matisse's parents mapped out his life for him. He attained a law degree and accepted a well-paid, secure job in a law office. But he decided to be an artist, not a lawyer, and threw all his energy into his ambition.

2 Define your problem

Define what you're trying to achieve. Matisse's problem was how to make an impact in the art world. What could he contribute to the field of painting to progress modern art?

Before starting a painting, Matisse asked himself what he wanted to express and how each work fitted with his next exhibition and longer-term goals. He decided to develop Van Gogh's use of intense, saturated colour to an extreme.

Matisse researched the history of art and contemporary art. He met all the leading artists of his time from Picasso to Cézanne, visited their studios, and interrogated them about their methods. He went to see all the galleries and collectors to try to work out where he could contribute to art. Ask yourself what you can add to your sphere.

3 Create ideas

Designers and artists generate many alternative ideas. To get ideas for a painting, Matisse tried out ideas in small sketches or small rough paintings.

When Matisse was creatively blocked, he'd change mediums, change subject matter or move somewhere inspiring. He'd even move to another country to get ideas from a different culture. He visited southern France to find inspiration and filled his paintings with bright colours and light, which led to one of his significant advances, the movement called 'Fauves' (wild beasts). Matisse travelled to Italy, Spain, North Africa and many other locations to re-energize his work. The more influences he discovered, the more successful he became.

Matisse never stopped developing new techniques. At the age of eighty-four, he experimented with coloured paper cut-outs of expressive human figures several metres in size. They were his most successful work.

4 Prototype

Prototyping is the experimental phase of producing many inexpensive, scaled-down versions of an idea to see what problems crop up, and then find solutions to them. A prototype enables you to test and evaluate a new idea on a small scale.

Before starting a large painting, Matisse produced tens of sketches and small pictures. He made original versions but on a manageable scale. Then he'd transfer ideas to a larger canvas.

As I've mentioned, Matisse was originally a lawyer. But he was dissatisfied and began attending drawing classes early in the morning before going to the office. Then he began experimenting with painting and sculpture. He prototyped a new career in a small way before committing himself.

There has never been a better time to prototype your ideas, in pop-up stores, podcasts, crowdfunding, blogs, Instagram . . . It's never been cheaper or easier to manufacture a product.

5 Test

Designers and artists test their work whenever they present it to the public. An exhibition was a way of seeing how favourably people reacted, and Matisse was attentive to feedback from critics, using it to assess whether to alter his work.

A student at one of my workshops worked in HR for a big company but was dissatisfied. We applied Design Thinking. I asked her to imagine she was sacked tomorrow and devise three alternative lives, no matter how far-fetched or risky. She was passionate about cooking and, in particular, virgin olive oil. Her fantasy was to produce her own brand of olive oil. We searched the internet and found a tiny olive grove for sale in Greece. She bought it online cheaply without even visiting. She discovered the locals harvested the olives for each other and kindly included her small plot. In London, she designed a bottle and label, drove to Greece to bottle the oil, filled her car, returned to London, and sold them in upmarket stores. A significant store gave her a concession, and with the profits and huge advance orders, she bought another small plot and then another. Soon she owned hundreds of acres, quit her job, and lived her ideal life (though it involved a lot of hard work). She'd still be stuck in a rut if she hadn't prototyped on a small scale. It gave her the confidence to scale up.

If you let things happen to you, you are not in control. Design your life, and you are guiding and shaping it. Like Matisse, think of your career and life as something that has to be crafted and sculpted. Keep the momentum of your career moving upwards and forwards.

Turn a 'no' into a 'yes'

We have all found ourselves like gladiators in the Roman arena waiting for the emperor to give a thumbs up to our application, proposal or pitch. While the reactive wait when they should act, the proactive do something – anything – to get the thumbs up. They take responsibility for their life and work, and throw everything at getting a 'yes'.

An idea grew in the mind of Tim Smit: a global garden. Built in Cornwall, England, the Eden Project would be housed in gigantic tropical biomes hundreds of metres in diameter. But it needed £56 million to fund. He applied for funding to the only source in England for such a huge grant, the Millennium Commission. It was a big, radical idea, but public committees prefer small, safe ideas. After a few weeks, Smit discovered his proposal was bottom of the four considered and was likely to get a thumbs down, so he was proactive and said he went to 'as dangerous a place as possible': he held a press conference to announce that the Millennium Commission had approved the funding. The media went into a frenzy, and *The Times* praised the Commission for backing an exciting project. It meant the Commission would have had to backtrack out of a commitment everyone thought they'd made. Smit said, 'It took about six weeks for the Commission to believe that they had said yes.' The Eden Project was built, hailed as the Eighth Wonder of the World, and attracts over a million visitors each year.

The proactive make things happen, but the reactive let things happen to them. Don't react. Be proactive. Take responsibility and do whatever is necessary to turn your ideas into reality.

Dr Charles Kelman wrote a grant proposal to advance cataract surgery. He woke up 'in the middle of the night, and, almost in a trance, added an addendum to my application that would affect the rest of my life and the lives of 100 million patients'.

He claimed he would 'develop a method for removing a cataract through an incision small enough so that no hospitalization will be required'. Who could resist such a claim? They awarded him the three-year grant. But he privately admitted, 'I did not have the vaguest idea of how to realize my idea.'

Kelman made his claim in response to an eminent ophthalmologist who asserted, 'Cataract surgery has been developed to its ultimate state, and any improvements from this date will be insignificant.' To a creative mind like Kelman, stating no further progress was possible was a red rag to a bull. Tell a creative thinker something is impossible, and they'll find a way to do it.

In my workshops for hospitals, I teach doctors, medical students and surgeons to be more innovative. It starts with a mindset of not being satisfied with the way things are and setting yourself a challenge, an unreasonable target. Wherever there is progress in medicine, it's due to a creative doctor prepared to challenge the orthodox approach.

Cataract surgery in the 1960s was an invasive procedure. The eye needed many stitches, and patients stayed in hospital for days. Using a similar approach to an artist, Kelman tried a range of experiments. Using animal eyes, he captured the cataract in a folding lens bag, crushed it, used rotating devices, high-speed cutting needles, a small blender, drills, small meat grinders and engraving tools. Nothing worked.

Kelman was visiting his dentist to have his teeth whitened when he became curious about the ultrasound probe. The dentist explained that its high-frequency vibration removed tartar without disturbing the tooth itself. Kelman jumped out of the chair and returned an hour later with a vitrine containing an eye with a cataractous lens. The ultrasound broke up the cataract.

Kelman perfected the technique and taught it to other ophthalmologists. The patients required no eye patches after surgery, no injections, only eye drops as an anaesthetic, and could walk out of the hospital immediately after the procedure. Kelman transformed the lives of millions.

1   Be prepared to do whatever is necessary to make your project happen, or don't start. Only do it if you believe it's worthwhile. Smit threw everything he had into the fight for the Eden Project. If you think your project is meaningful, useful and contributes something significant, nothing will hold you back.

2   Don't let 'no' be the final word. The proactive focus on things they can do. The reactive waste energy on something they have no control over. Working out where to expend your energy for maximum impact is the first important step towards getting a thumbs up.

3   Anticipate people's objections before they raise them and steer them towards a 'yes'. Often people say 'no' because it's the most comfortable option – they're worried the risk might affect their job.

4   Be persuasive, not persistent. The saying 'never take no for an answer' is mistakenly understood as 'pester people until they say yes'. If you do that, you'll only reinforce their 'no' response. Discover why they're saying 'no' so you can find the way to turn it into a 'yes'.

Sell yourself without selling out

I couldn't believe my luck. On my first day in New York in the 80s, I was at a private view in a downtown gallery, and Andy Warhol was a guest. He was a great historic artist but also the artist I most admired. It was a once in a lifetime opportunity, and I felt compelled to go up and tell him how much I admired his work. I had been in awe of him since I'd first become interested in art. Warhol's influence is everywhere, from his regularly copied pop art paintings to films, magazines and his prophetic 'In the future everyone will be famous for fifteen minutes' quote.

I was over in New York at the invitation of a gallery that was showing my paintings. On another evening, at a party in a club, incredibly, Warhol was there. Then a couple of evenings later, he was at another private view. He seemed to be everywhere. I was surprised at how a famous workaholic like Warhol was at almost every function.

Warhol's assistants told me he wasn't partying, he was working at soliciting portrait commissions. Going to parties, private views and clubs was work. Warhol wasn't selling himself, he was offering a useful service. His offer? 'I can do a great portrait of you.'

Warhol was working – or more precisely, networking. He was looking for opportunities to meet collectors, film directors or stars. He was an artist whose work was already assured a place in history, yet he was out late every night networking. I should have been the one networking hard as I was unknown in New York.

The term 'self-promotion' makes everyone cringe. We're all irritated by pushy, overbearing people. We all have to network and promote our work, but no one wants to come across as self-obsessed, insincere and phony. What if you feel uncomfortable blowing your own trumpet? Networking can feel embarrassing and painful to do in a way that feels authentic. So be authentic. Don't think of networking as finding people who'll help you. Think of networking as finding people you can help. To explain why what you're offering is worthwhile, you need to be sure in your mind what is unique about it.

Networking is difficult because most of us aren't pushy. Thinking about helping others takes you out of yourself. You're thinking outwards rather than inwards. Go to networking events with an aim: work out what you have to offer – then offer it. What can you do for them? Most people tell people what they do and how but forget to explain why. Don't think of it as a pitch, or you'll start to think of yourself as a salesman.

The elevator pitch is a concise, compelling, persuasive explanation of what makes your work, product or idea unique, told in the thirty or forty seconds it takes the elevator to reach the floor of the person you're pitching to. It's easier if you can sum it up in one or two sentences: what problems you solve and how you could help them. More importantly, these sentences help you clarify in your mind what you're trying to achieve. What's in it for them?

1   Go to a networking event with the intention of helping others. People will notice if you're pushing yourself and it's a turn-off. Explain why what you do is worthwhile and what you can do for them.

2   Warhol created introverted ways to do extroverted things. He didn't say much but let the other person speak; he was genuinely interested in them. He didn't become a fake extrovert, but found a different way of achieving his aims. He was a good listener and noted ways he could add value to people's work. A genuine listener is rare, which is why people warm to them. Warhol was curious, attentive and easy-going. Listen more, talk less.

3   Don't feel under pressure to say something funny or clever. Warhol used to smile a lot and say little more than 'Wow!' occasionally. He put people at their ease, and his calmness gave him a presence and an aura of gravitas.

Put what is in your mind into the world

One day, Verner Panton had a brilliant idea for a chair: the back, seat and legs would be one continuous fluid shape that fitted the human body perfectly. It would be the first chair moulded entirely from one single substance. Within a few minutes, he'd sketched the voluptuous curves. It was also highly practical, and easy to stack and to clean.

The inspiration was the easy bit. Panton spent years trying different materials and produced tens of unsuccessful prototypes. They were either too rigid and snapped, or too flexible. Panton tried to get technical help. 'Fifteen to twenty manufacturers have tried it but have all rejected the project for different reasons,' he recalled. Many manufacturers and technicians even told him it was impossible. F. Scott Fitzgerald said, 'Genius is the ability to put into effect what is in your mind. There's no other definition of it.' Panton had to make his idea tangible.

Eventually, Panton teamed up with the manufacturer Vitra, and they worked together for almost two decades. After trying hundreds of different plastics, they discovered the perfect mix, firm yet springy – and thus the first moulded plastic chair was made.

When they first displayed the Panton chair in a shop window in New York in 1967, a huge crowd gathered and blocked the street. The Panton chair deserves the overused title 'design classic', because it's one of the twentieth century's most outstanding designs.

A designer called Gunnar Andersen was furious when he first saw the Panton chair. It was identical to his 1953 prototype made a few months before Panton had the idea. Andersen had produced prototypes in aluminium and other materials, but soon gave up. Both he and Panton had had the same concept, but Panton put what was in his mind into the world; Andersen didn't.

1   'If the fool would persist in his folly he would become wise,' said William Blake. Persist with your idea. People give up before they have brought out the true potential of their concept. Inspiration is a glamorous and exciting aspect of creativity, but only stamina will transform an idea into reality.

2   Learn to enjoy the barriers to success. Successful creative people are not the ones with the most talent, but the ones who see their work to realization. A novel, album, exhibition, setting up a business or completing a scientific project is a marathon, not a sprint. Tenacity has a lot to do with overcoming the inner doubts that have been put in your mind by education, parents or society. Panton relished overcoming the technical obstacles and also his internal blocks.

3   There's a myth that tenacity is something you're either born with or you're not. This isn't true. You can consciously cultivate it, and it's an essential quality to push yourself to your full potential. Relentlessly pursuing a goal could make others jealous and uncomfortable because they lack the same determination, but Panton could look back on his achievement and see it wasn't down to luck or inherited wealth but maintaining composure when things went persistently wrong.

4   Any creative endeavour is a test of your grit and resilience. 'Don't assume you know how much potential you have. Sometimes the only way to know what you can do is to test yourself,' said Scott Adams, creator of the Dilbert comic strip.

Four ways to create 'stickiness'

Much of what we see is instantly forgettable. Biology teachers explain fascinating subjects like genetically engineered plants that fight pollution, but it comes across as dull and instantly forgettable. A manager explains a new, radical strategy in a PowerPoint presentation that no one can recall. You go to an art exhibition, walk around baffled, and can't wait to get out.

How do you get your work to stick to people's minds like a barnacle to a boat?

Whether it's a business, novel, concert or exhibition, your work will only be successful if it stays in people's minds. Human memory is like a wax block – if something has made an impression, it remains.

Frank Gehry received a commission to design a building to promote cutting-edge research into the treatment of degenerative brain diseases. Diseases like Alzheimer's were unfashionable areas of medicine back in 2010, so a landmark building in Las Vegas was needed to put brain disease at the forefront of the medical world and attract the best scientific minds. Gehry explained, 'I'm trying to make a building that people will want to visit, remember, talk about and enjoy, and ultimately will persuade them to want to partner with us to help cure some of the neurodegenerative diseases.'

Gehry combined great architecture with a great purpose, and he succeeded in his aim: the building's high profile made the most significant medical minds from around the world want to be involved in the project. And his dilemma was one we all face: how do you produce something memorable?

If your project is worthwhile, you need to get your message across and make it stick. The problem architects face in Las Vegas is that it's already full of shiny, exciting new buildings, but when confronted by the Lou Ruvo Center there, your reaction is, 'What the hell is that?!' The contorted, sweeping stainless steel of the building draws fascinated crowds and is impossible to ignore. Like a good novel, it grabs your attention, and then the unfolding plot keeps you intrigued. The impressive design has 'stickiness' and is an easily understood metaphor for Alzheimer's.

If you want to communicate with someone effectively you have to speak to their heart as well as their head. Someone has to become

emotionally attached to your message for it to stick. Everyone who sees the Lou Ruvo Center wants to go inside and see if its interior is as brilliant as the outside. The centre is a useful marketing device, raising awareness for its valuable research.

Scientist Carl Sagan had a similar problem with an urgent NASA mission. Once every 175 years, Jupiter, Saturn, Uranus and Neptune align, and in the late 70s, it was about to happen. It was essential to immediately send the probe *Voyager 1* to collect data from all the planets, but American politicians wouldn't approve funding. It wasn't a vote-winning project because another scientific probe collecting more data was not memorable.

So Sagan had an idea: the Golden Record, a message to aliens on a phonograph record (gold-plated for protection) attached to *Voyager 1*.

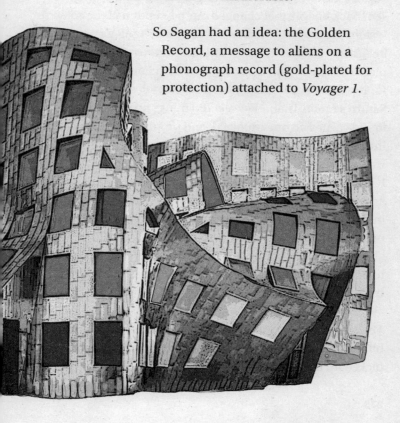

The Golden Record communicated the story of Earth to extra-terrestrials and contained sounds, music, images showing human life and culture, and greetings from people in fifty-five languages. The public was fascinated.

The Golden Record inspired the world to ask what was important to us and what we would like to tell extra-terrestrials. It was not just talking to aliens, but also to humanity. Imagining an extra-terrestrial listening to our music, reading our poems and looking at our pictures made the public see things from other perspectives.

Sagan's idea worked, and NASA got the funding. *Voyager 1* sent back images that changed our perception of the solar system. It discovered active volcanoes on Jupiter's moon, the intricacies of Saturn's rings, multiple moons on the four outer planets, lightning on a planet other than Earth, an ocean on Jupiter's moon Europa, and a nitrogen-rich atmosphere on Saturn's moon Titan. '*Voyager* did things no one predicted, found scenes no one expected, and promises to outlive its inventors,' said author Stephen J. Pyne.

It's often not enough to plop information in front of people and tell them why they should support you; you have to inspire and capture imaginations. Many years later, Sagan reflected on the Golden Record, 'One thing would be clear about us: no one sends such a message on such a journey, to other worlds and beings, without a positive passion for the future.'

Voyager 1 has now travelled beyond the solar system and is billions of miles into interstellar space. Perhaps an alien has picked up its signal as you read this.

Here are four strategies to make your ideas sticky:

1 Be straightforward. Why are proverbs so memorable? Because they're concise, short, and tell a story in a few sentences. A lawyer sums up his case to the jury at the end of a trial with one argument. He may have ten, but if he tells each one of them to the jury, he knows they'll forget them all in the jury room. It's difficult to discard lots of compelling information if you have a product with many attributes and you want to declare them, but the lawyer has to distil information down to one key fact – and so do you.

2 Remember the element of surprise. The unexpected attracts attention, so create a surprising message to make your work stand out from the background noise. Exceptional work is shared and remembered.

3 Provoke emotion. Make people feel something. Warmth. Disgust. Fascination. Anger. Connect with people through their feelings because that establishes rapport.

4 Create a story. A story is more engaging than a matter-of-fact explanation. The story of the Golden Record fascinated people because they imagined what they would put on it – what they personally thought were the important landmarks of world culture.

Don't join the navy, be a pirate

If you're going to pirate music, don't target giants like the Beatles or Jay-Z, with their teams of lawyers and financial muscle. Brian Burton (Danger Mouse) did exactly that. He mixed Jay-Z's *Black Album* with the Beatles' legendary *White Album* – a surreal fusion of two music icons. *The Grey Album* was a surprising phenomenon and named the best album of 2004 by *Entertainment Weekly*. Burton made sure everything was in sync: the moods, the tempos and the vocals are on the beat, and the backing fits with the lyrics, forcing us to view the two music giants in a new way. Burton was a fan of both Jay-Z and the Beatles, so why not mash them together? He pirated them, and copyright issues arose, but Jay-Z and McCartney loved the album and let it go.

A female pirate swaggered defiantly through London's streets sporting a tricorn hat, buccaneer boots and an eye patch. She brandished a fearful weapon – a pirate state of mind. Seventeenth-century pirates were not the drunken criminals portrayed in films. The government and naval hierarchy of the time treated sailors appallingly, so piracy was born out of rebellion against this treatment and the desire for a fairer system.

In a similar vein, our female pirate had a desire to change urban deprivation, climate change and the corporatization of everything. Her name was Vivienne Westwood, and it was the early 1980s. To achieve her aims, she used four essential methods:

Mutiny: Vivienne Westwood and her partner Malcolm McLaren took over a shop in the same spirit that pirates claim a ship, to run it their own way. The facade of the newly named Worlds End had a massive clock with hands spinning backwards, and like a pirate ship, you climbed aboard rickety wooden stairs and stepped onto a slanted floor like a galleon deck. There were racks of pirate clothes on either side.

When pirates took over ships, there was not the chaos depicted in movies. They ran them on democratic principles similar to today's unions. The captain's and crew members' earnings were shared equitably. Pirates' families were cared for if they were injured or died. 'Why join the navy if you can be a pirate?' said Apple founder Steve Jobs. Westwood ran Worlds End like a pirate captain, as a fusion of store, studio, gallery, stage and museum.

Philosophy: One afternoon in the 1980s, a German magazine called *Kunstmarkt* interviewed me. I had recently left college, but I'd only done a few interviews and was still trying to articulate my ideas. The journalist had interviewed Malcolm McLaren in the morning because he was launching a new rock group called Bow Wow Wow. They mixed high culture and mass culture, and various music styles – rock, Burundi, opera, South American . . . McLaren had explained his philosophy in a nutshell: take what you need from the past and different cultures, and mix them – postmodernism, in other words. He knew how to communicate his ideas clearly and succinctly.

Re-creation: Westwood dominated the fashion world by fusing clothes from different periods and cultures. She chose whatever most appealed to her: T-shirts with Grecian togas, conical bras worn over the top of ethnic African shirts, seventeenth-century French dresses beneath jackets made from South American boldly geometric textiles, and highwaymen's boots mashed together with the bowler hats of women from Bolivia. Westwood's clothing acknowledged the debt Western society owed to ethnic cultures, and was a greatest hits collection of what she considered the best from past and present around the world, sewn together with wit and wisdom.

Westwood and McLaren's first-ever catwalk collection in 1981 was titled 'Pirate', because it plundered the era of buccaneers with wide-bottomed striped buccaneer trousers, and extra-large shirts with sashes.

Put all the things you most admire into your work – no matter how diverse they are. Mix the best of your influences and create the greatest hits collection of your sphere, whether that's technology, engineering, art, music, cinema or business.

Collaboration: Treat your fans and customers like friends. At Worlds End, customers felt involved. Some of my friends were customers who hung out in the shop; they were offered jobs, and often made the clothes.

The modern navy has embraced the pirate mentality of welcoming new ideas from wherever and whoever. They are hungry for innovation, and appreciate the contribution of mavericks. If you want to be a pirate, join the navy.

Transform the insignificant into the significant

You won't always be lucky enough to work on significant projects for prominent organizations, galleries or film companies. If you have to work on an insignificant project, throw everything you've got at it as if it were highly prestigious. Don't think 'I'm not getting paid much' or 'Not many important people will see this, so it deserves little effort'; throw everything at it. It's down to you to turn an inconsequential project into something meaningful. With only a small budget, you'll need big dreams and creativity.

Could you point to Gagra in Abkhazia on a map? Probably not, but it's worth going because there's an extraordinary design there that you must see, and one that embodies an invaluable attitude. You'll be in for a long, arduous journey because it's one of the remotest places on earth, but your visit

Missed the bus

will teach you that it's possible to do your best work for the worst commission.

In the Soviet Union, architects like Zurab Tsereteli had to adhere to the authorities' strict, ultra-conservative guidelines. It resulted in schools, hospitals and government buildings that looked like bleak concrete prisons. Tons of painful bureaucratic policies, rigidly upheld by numerous committees, weighed down Soviet architects. 'It was practically impossible to express oneself,' said one such architect, Armen Sardarov. 'It was a time of monotony in architecture.' They had to use prefabricated concrete blocks with ready-made openings for doors and windows, which produced a pompous and colossal style called 'conservative monumentalism' – the stereotypical image we have of a Soviet city, with a miserly, utilitarian look that creates a grey and lifeless environment.

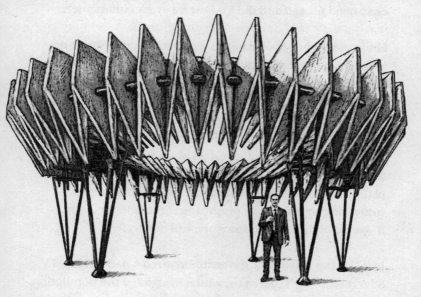

Drove the bus

Tsereteli received commissions to design bus shelters in remote villages like Gagra – the least prestigious projects with the lowest budgets. But the Soviet authorities would never see them, so they were a chance for creatively repressed architects to express themselves. Tsereteli revelled in this artistic freedom and threw all his inventiveness and creativity into the shelters. These unique structures are now presented as masterpieces in books on architecture. Photographers travel thousands of miles across the world's harshest deserts to photograph them. Tsereteli produced work of the highest quality and threw all his skills and abilities into the designs.

We must keep to our high standards – even when no one is looking. Ambition drives people to produce brilliant work, but it often leads to arrogance if they think a commission is beneath them. Zurab Tsereteli was ambitious, but he controlled his ego and did his best for every commission.

His beautiful bus shelters are a notable legacy of Soviet-era architecture, still lovingly maintained by the local populations. Look at the bus shelters where you live. Are they beautiful, architectural masterpieces?

If you're working on an insignificant project, exhibiting in a provincial gallery, writing for an obscure magazine or performing in a small bar, don't do it half-heartedly. It's a platform. Transform an insignificant commission into something significant by producing something brilliant. If you do brilliant work, someone will notice.

In 2012, the Taiwanese government aired a patronizing TV advert entitled 'Trust in us', which instructed the population not to 'waste time questioning their policies' and to get on with their work. A group of computer programmers was infuriated, and they started a tech-centred revolution. Among their number was transgender student Audrey Tang, who'd had to drop out of junior high school early because of the prejudice she'd suffered. Things had not looked promising for Tang, but she rose to become one of the most prominent members of the group that became known as The Sunflower Revolution.

The group made copies of the government's websites but redesigned them to reveal how they spent public money – a practice that was christened 'forking'. They were not trying to undermine the government, however, but to improve it. Hired hands designed government websites, and because they didn't care, the sites were dull and shoddy. But the activists cared about helping the public and getting the truth out. They quadruple checked all their facts to ensure they were accurate, and made their sites user-friendly. Their sites drew hundreds of thousands of visitors, and The Sunflower Revolution grew into a powerful force. Eventually, the Taiwanese government had to listen. To their credit, they saw the potential and started to work with these 'revolutionaries'.

In 2016, Tang was given the significant role of minister without portfolio. A high-school dropout, hacker and protestor had become the youngest and first transgender minister in the world. By doing brilliant work for a small fringe movement, she was able to bring about radical reforms to Taiwan's government. It led to a new concept of democracy, and the Taiwanese government became respected as the most transparent in the world. Tang's example shows us that we live in a culture where we can empower ourselves.

My big break in the art world came from entering a print in an obscure exhibition in Leeds. The eminent art critic Edward Lucie-Smith happened to see it and asked to look at more of my work, before writing a glowing review of my first solo exhibition in *The Times*. As a result, every painting sold.

1	See the potential for creativity in even the smallest opportunities. Do any task as well as possible. As a freelance illustrator, I often worked on a small commission for a magazine for little money, but I put everything I had into making it great. Art directors noticed and hired me to do lucrative advertising projects. Putting a lot of drive, energy and effort into a small commission impresses people and they wonder, 'What would they do with a bigger project?'

2	Make an insignificant commission significant by producing something brilliant. Please don't dismiss it as a waste of time and wait for a prestigious project. This is it! It's easy to become confused by the tangled mess of budgets, opinions, financial incentives and other pressures. We feel the best course of action in our gut, and we must follow that feeling.

'The most personal is the most creative'

Products and services with the same features, same price and quality surround us. How do you make your work distinctive and brilliant?

When Bong Joon-ho received the Oscar for best director, he explained that when he was at film school, he came across a quote from Martin Scorsese that 'I carved deep into my heart, which is, "the most personal is the most creative".' Joon-ho's film, *Parasite*, was a low-budget Korean thriller that swept the biggest prizes at the 92nd Academy Awards, making history for a non-English-language film. Joon-ho's personality filled the entire film, and Scorsese's quote should be carved onto everyone's heart because it's relevant in every field.

Adopt an 'auteur' mindset. 'Auteur' describes a film director like Quentin Tarantino, Andrei Tarkovsky or David Lynch. Their films stand out from the crowd because although a movie is a team effort, their vision imbues them with meaning and style. They apply personal themes to every aspect of their work, and they are the film's authors in the same way that an author writes a novel: they take responsibility for every character, plotline and everything that appears on the screen. Every artist, entrepreneur, scientist or businessperson should think of themselves as an auteur.

An auteur thinks deeply about how they perceive the world, and how they share this vision with others. They analyse every aspect of their work and get to the core of issues. Shallow thinking leads to shallow work, and a shallow thinker is content with stating the obvious. Auteurs analyse and examine every aspect of what they see, read or hear, and the same is true of any artwork, project or service you deliver.

Being an auteur is not about stamping a style on something, but letting your deeper values affect your work. A film director on set is an extreme version of all our lives; they're in a high-pressure situation with constant distractions, bombarded by people giving their opinions. It's easy to lose your way. But they have a deep understanding of what they're trying to do.

The most enduring, successful films have an instantly recognizable, personal director's stamp. Kubrick, Coppola, Tarantino, Wes Anderson, Robert Altman and Peter Bogdanovich have such unique styles that you can identify one of their movies after a few seconds. They fought the movie studios to ensure committees and accountants didn't reduce their eccentric, original films into insipid, bland mush. The studio approach made filmmaking into a committee process designed to make money; consequently, studio films often lack individuality.

Musician Kanye West is the overall director of every aspect of his creative process. He writes the material, supervises the arrangements, masterminds every phase of the recording process and often takes creative control of his music videos. He had the same approach when he worked on clothing with brands Louis Vuitton, Nike and Adidas. He's won twenty-one Grammys because his work is immediately identifiable.

Similarly, Jenny Fleiss and Jennifer Hyman stamped their personalities on their multimillion-pound internet business Rent the Runway. When they were students, they had an inspiring vision – access was more important than ownership. Their mission was to reshape the clothes market. Most people rarely wear most of their clothes, and they end up at the back of wardrobes or in landfill. Their idea was that you rent clothes instead and expand the sharing economy. Their vision 'Buy less. Own more. Be you' radiates through their business.

1   Gain as deep an understanding of yourself as possible. The deeper you know yourself, the more you'll understand what you want to produce.

2   Resolve to take responsibility for every aspect of your work and become its auteur. Leave your stamp on everything. Don't give in to pressure to become 'something else'. To have a long career and be in demand, you need to develop your distinctive voice. It's not about being a control freak but developing a vision.

3   If you're doing things thoroughly, your work will have your personality. If it doesn't, you're not involved enough in it.

Don't be controlled by others

We can find ourselves controlled by the opinions of others.
What others think about us and our work can start to matter
more than what we believe, and social media amplifies
this feeling.

There's a technique for listening to your authentic inner self.
It enables you to deal with anxiety and a low sense of self-
esteem, and helps you develop the ability to monitor your
emotions. Notice how you react to the opinions of others and
use your observations to learn how to handle disappointment.
Develop the skill of letting go of negative feelings and practise
empowering emotions. To be authentic, we need to be
independent of the praise of others.

The film director William Friedkin released *The French
Connection* in 1971 and knew after the first day that it was a
box office hit, and he would be a millionaire. He achieved
his dream of winning an Oscar, and the night was a whirl of
parties and press interviews. The following day he visited a
psychiatrist for the first time because the award plunged him
into deep feelings of emptiness. The psychiatrist listened in
silence for an hour, then Friedkin left and never returned.
Friedkin realized the only reward was his satisfaction in the
work. Gratification will only come from producing work you
think is brilliant. He went on to direct *The Exorcist* to even
greater success.

If you enter awards, you feel crushed if you don't win. But if you do succeed, there's a sense of anti-climax. Approval has to come from inside you, not from outside. Soon after I graduated from the Royal College of Art, I entered my work for a prestigious award. The previous winners were all artists I had tremendous respect for, and I was sure that being the next winner would give me some validation. I won. The evening was a blur of significant people in the industry congratulating me and shaking my hand. My friends were all excited and wanted to go out and celebrate. The prize money, commissions and attention were useful, but the award didn't give me any sense of fulfilment because nothing external gives you any real satisfaction.

In *A Theory of Human Motivation*, psychologist Abraham Maslow identifies our hierarchy of needs. Once we have fulfilled our basic needs – food, shelter and a supportive network of friends – the highest level of psychological development is self-actualization. The self-actualized realize they have a duty to express their potential. They disregard the opinions of others and live in whatever way is most fulfilling. 'A musician must make music, an artist must paint, a poet must write if he is to be ultimately happy,' Maslow says. Some examples of the self-actualized might be a painter who paints because it's fulfilling, even though it makes them little money; a woman who enjoys quilt-making even though it's regarded as a lowly craft by the art world; or a worker in a not-for-profit charity who uses their skills to help others. It's an appealing quality in a culture where people are more anxious to get 'likes' than to express their real values.

Maslow gives other examples in his book from a wide range of occupations – from athletes to philosophers, scientists to artists. He points out an early feminist, Jane Addams, who was a pacifist who fought for women's right to vote. She was fulfilled because she established what mattered most to her and pursued her interest with assurance. Despite a barrage of criticism from the press and public, she withstood the pressure. Her inner moral compass kept her on course. When she was awarded the Nobel Peace Prize, she dealt with the adulation in an equally level-headed way.

1   See your ultimate goal not as awards, but as the drive to actualize your full personal potential. To do this, you need to determine what makes you feel most fulfilled and pursue it relentlessly no matter what others think.

2   Striving for validation and awards leads you astray. Prizes are useful to attract publicity to your work, in the way that winning an Oscar attracts attention to a film, but don't expect awards to give you any sense of lasting satisfaction or self-worth. Enter awards, but whether you win or lose, turn your attention to the next steps. Looking to the future will help take your mind off the achievement and refocus on what you are trying to build.

If you don't know what to do, use the six 'W's

Sometimes we're burning with desire to do something worthwhile but don't know what or where to begin.

The solution is the six 'W's. They clarify **WHAT** you want to do and **WHY**. The Greek philosopher Aristotle devised them for everyone, but they're popular with authors, musicians and artists. Journalists, scientists and police investigators also use the six 'W's, because they are essential problem-solving tools. Aristotle believed ignorance of just one of the six 'W's could lead to personal calamity. There are six critical questions, with the final question being the most important.

Mary and Alexander were a great example of people who used the six 'W's to achieve international success; their gut instincts led them right along that path.

1 Who

Mary and Alexander knew **WHO** they were. They were not nine to fivers but free spirits who could never do a desk job. Although they had little finance, they knew they were entrepreneurial and trusted their gut instincts. It's surprising how many successful entrepreneurs, scientists and artists reveal their secret is 'trusting their gut'. If things went wrong, it was because they listened to advice from accountants, managers or banks, 'even though it didn't feel right'.

* Interrogate yourself. Find out **WHO** you are. Superficial self-knowledge leads to a shallow life, so don't move forward until you know.

2 What

Mary and Alexander knew they wanted to do something brilliant. But they didn't know **WHAT**. They had drive and ambition, but **WHAT** to do with it? The only way for them to discover **WHAT**, was to do. They considered starting a café, then a jazz club, but decided to open a shop. They had no retail experience, but Mary was interested in clothing. They had established their **WHAT**.

* **WHAT** do you genuinely care about most? Pursue your most vital interest, even if it means struggling financially at first.

3 Where

Mary and Alexander knew **WHERE** they wanted to be – in Chelsea, London. In the early 1960s England was a grey place, suffering from post-war austerity, but unlike the rest of England, Chelsea was exciting and adventurous. They fed off its energy and opened a boutique there called Bazaar, selling clothes and accessories.

* Your environment affects your well-being and can either energize you or leave you drained. Choose **WHERE** to live and work carefully.

4 When

In 60s Britain, clothes were old-fashioned and the fabrics were drab. Mary sensed Britain was ready for new ideas, and her designs declared, 'Change is coming'. She felt restricted by the limited styles available to her and assumed other women felt the same. It was the perfect time for a new, modern look.

* Develop a sense for new ideas emerging at the cutting edge of culture, technology and values. Immerse yourself in them.

5 With

WITH is about the techniques and materials you'll use to develop your **WHAT**.

Wholesalers didn't believe Mary was a businessperson and wouldn't sell to her. On the opening day of her shop, many of the shelves and hangers were bare. Hats were expensive, so Mary started making her own designs. The clothes she wanted didn't exist, so she made them. She bought a sewing machine, struggled with it, then hired a dressmaker to help her – then another and another.

Mary decided she didn't like the standard shop window mannequins standing grandly with one toe pointed. She wanted contemporary figures **WITH** modern haircuts and real-life poses. She hired a sculptor to make some for her. They were hugely expensive, but they had a dramatic impact.

WITH no finance, Mary had to hold her first catwalk show in her shop. The models danced into the showroom to jazz music, wearing her inventive designs. One model carried a shotgun, another a book by Karl Marx, and another swung a dead pheasant around – unintentionally spattering blood around the room, on the walls and on the journalists. Now, it's commonplace for catwalk shows to be a mixture of theatre and performance art, but it was entirely original at the time.

✳ Work out **WHAT** materials and techniques you will use. Financial resources are not as crucial as inventive and innovative methods.

6 Why

The Mary of this chapter has been, of course, the legendary fashion designer Mary Quant. 'I had always wanted the young to have fashion of their own . . . absolutely twentieth-century fashion . . . but I knew nothing about the fashion business,' she said. She had a cause and a purpose for designing clothes. Everything Mary made stemmed from her **WHY**. Everyone working for her was passionate because they knew **WHY** they were doing what they were doing.

Think strategically, act tactically

If you want to get a plan approved by your boss, get a novel published or get a gallery's backing, you need both strategy and tactics. When you begin any new venture, enter a meeting or start a new job, think strategically and act tactically. We all fall into the trap of forgetting to work out what we want from a situation and don't work out a strategy or act tactically.

Two thousand five hundred years ago, Chinese military strategist Sun Tzu wrote a book called *The Art of War*, which is still a bestseller. He said, 'Strategy without tactics is the slowest route to victory. Tactics without strategy is the noise before defeat.' It's imperative to be sure your tactics and your strategy work together.

Strategy defines your long-term goal, your destination; tactics are the practical steps you take to get there.

A brilliant strategy is about defining your priorities, focusing on the goal, understanding the system.

Brilliant tactics outline the tasks and timeline needed to reach that goal. The right tactics are tangible, immediate actions.

An artwork called *Strategies* represents the art world's structure: a house of cards made from copies of the magazine *Flash Art* that dominated the art world. A review in *Flash Art* got you noticed. *Strategies* was a precarious structure on the verge of collapse. It was artist Maurizio Cattelan's comment on the mechanics of the art scene and it showed how he'd analysed the structure of the art world system. As a relatively unknown artist, he worked out how he could infiltrate it. When Cattelan arrived in Milan in 1990, he was a complete unknown in the Italian art world, which was a closed shop for someone like him with no art school training or contacts. He thought long and hard about how to make an impact. The usual route an artist would take – publications, critical approval, galleries – wasn't open. He said, 'Instead of waiting for *Flash Art* to notice me, I thought I would put my own work on the cover.' He photographed *Strategies*, pasted the photo onto the cover of various editions of *Flash Art* and distributed them to shops. He established himself as the joker of the art world who questioned its relevance to everyday life.

Cattelan's strategy was to become accepted as an artist. His tactics were the subversive steps he took to infiltrate museums and institutions.

Cattelan's works are an irreverent attack on art institutions. He gained worldwide notoriety in New York with *La Nona Ora* (*The Ninth Hour*), a realistic statue of Pope John Paul II hit by a meteorite. In 2011, Maurizio Cattelan had a solo exhibition at the Guggenheim Museum in New York and suspended all his works from the ceiling. For a year, in the Guggenheim's restroom, he installed a fully functional toilet made of 18-carat gold, available for the public to use.

An understanding of strategy and tactics helps anyone creative achieve their goals. Artists have always been tactical, embracing new methods that are cheap and don't require expensive materials, lots of assistants or huge studios.

A large group of supervisors and managers watched sceptically as a softball pitcher threw beanbags across a checkout scanner as fast as possible. The situation had been tactically devised by George Laurer to get around obstacles in the organization he worked for.

In the 70s, Laurer was broke. Before job interviews, he had to go to the police station to ask if he could wash in the bathroom. He landed a job at IBM. His first task did not seem to have much potential, but when he realized the inventory management was inefficient, he decided to find a better way to track groceries. By thinking tactically, Laurer saw an opportunity to make a significant impact.

A supervisor asked Laurer to devise a code of circular symbols to track packaging. It had to fit on awkwardly shaped products, be under an inch and a half, and be legible to humans and machines. Laurer's problem was how to get a radical new idea around his supervisors and the bureaucracy of IBM. 'I struggled a day or two, but my nature and training would not allow me to support something I did not believe in,' he wrote in his memoir.

Cattelan used strategy to make an impact in the art world; Laurer did the same at IBM. You can get lost in a maze of paperwork and meetings in a huge organization, so use strategy to make an impression. Laurer decided against circles and invented a row of stripes with varying widths and spacing. He said, 'I simply went against my manager's instruction and set out to design a better system.' He challenged the system but tactically. 'I was truly playing "bet your job" by designing a new code rather than supporting what the brass wanted,' he said.

He realized he had to make his idea, then prove it worked. If he had asked permission he could have got bogged down in meetings and admin, so he set up the beanbag demonstration to prove his method. His immediate boss made it clear that if the top brass didn't like his barcode, he'd lose his job. The beanbags had Laurer's code label on the bottom, the scanner read them, and the division head approved.

IBM's barcodes were first used by the grocery industry in 1973 and quickly spread across the world to identify objects in stores, warehouses, anywhere; on aeroplane parts, toll-road booths, parking tickets, and blood packets in hospitals. Laurer later helped develop handheld wands for scanning codes. He created a revolution in merchandising by using strategy to get around his boss and IBM's bureaucracy.

1   To infiltrate a system, understand and devise your tactics and strategy. 'Artists defy authority,' said playwright Timberlake Wertenbaker. 'If you accept authority and orthodoxy, you cannot be creative. The whole point of being an artist is to look beyond received ideas and to question them.' That's true of artists and anyone who wants to be creative.

2   Write down your strategy (the bigger picture) and your tactics (what steps you'll take next).

To be understood, speak directly

How do you get a project off to a good start? It's hard to stop your thoughts going down the same old tramlines and regurgitating old ideas. You want new thoughts that shoot off in exciting new directions and take you to places you've never dreamt of. Ask yourself who you most want to astonish, either a real person or someone who is typical of your audience. A songwriter might want to write a song John Lennon would appreciate, for example; an artist could wish for Frida Kahlo's approval; a politician might want to earn Nelson Mandela's respect. Visualize someone who you admire and produce work to gain his or her admiration. Think of it as asking advice from someone who has values you respect.

Designers were obsessed with neomania in the 1970s. Looking backward meant you were backward. Then a chair appeared that looked backward and forward at the same time. Designer Alessandro Mendini asked himself what chair design would amaze the writer Marcel Proust if he were still alive. Born in 1871, Proust is considered the first modern novelist, and Mendini visited places from Proust's life to understand his values and use them to get inspiration. Mendini smashed the ornamental neo-baroque style of eighteenth-century France together with minimalist modern art to create the first masterpiece of postmodern design. Mendini intended the chair to be a one-off experiment, but it struck a chord in the design world. Its popularity forced him to create many thousands more in ceramic, bronze and marble. It was a success because it was designed to impress someone who was hard to impress.

William Friedkin is the director of award-winning box office successes like *The Exorcist* and *The French Connection*. He made films for his uncle who worked in a deli in Chicago because it meant 'I have my finger on the pulse of America', and his films spoke to millions. He could ask himself, could they relate to this, will they laugh, be entertained, bored? Aim at one well-chosen person in particular and your message will hit many targets.

It's a myth that artists only do work to please themselves. This book contains my personal views and ideas, but I want people to read it. It costs a fortune to print and distribute. I need a publisher to help me, and they deserve a cut for their hard work. When I wrote my first book, I pictured one of my art students, and what would be useful to them. But I hoped it would also appeal to people in business, science, and other art forms looking to inject creative thinking into their organizations – fortunately it did, and became a bestseller.

You can talk to yourself, shout strident views out of the window, or communicate your ideas to an audience who appreciates and relates to them. Wallowing in your own artistic self-satisfaction is self-indulgent. Put your ego in a box and deliver something useful. A Rothko painting is helpful because the viewer realizes someone else feels the same deep moods as them. 'You're not the only one who feels that way,' his paintings seem to say, empathizing with those who feel lost and dejected. 'I've been there too.' Even abstract paintings have a purpose and use.

Have you ever read a book and thought, *this author expressed the feelings I thought were unique to me*. Art can make you feel understood when the world makes you feel misunderstood. 'I used to think I was the strangest person in the world, but then I thought there are so many people in the world, there must be someone just like me who feels bizarre and flawed in the same ways I do,' Frida Kahlo once said. I often get emails from readers who express the same sentiments to me, and it's good to feel that connection, that we're in this together. It's a deep form of communication when we read a book and realize that the author has pinpointed our thoughts and feelings.

1   When kicking off a project, have someone specific
in mind – someone whose values you trust. Talk directly to
them. Think of them as a respected friend you're chatting to,
and your work is the conversation. Your tone will seem more
casual, as if you're speaking one-to-one with them, rather than
to a faceless crowd. Speak to everyone, and you'll talk to no
one. If you have a fuzzy, vague vision of your audience, your
work will be blurred and ambiguous. Don't start talking until
you know who you're talking to.

2   Empathize with your audience. When Steve Jobs
launched the iPod, the tech industry's attitude was 'so what?'
MP3 players were nothing new. Everyone had one. The
difference was the way Jobs described the iPod. Other tech
companies were explaining their MP3 player as having '2 GB of
storage!' Or '3 GB!' Jobs said, '1,000 songs in your pocket,' and
the phrase created a picture you could relate to. Be sure you
only do work that has meaning for you – it's the only way you'll
have the passion to convey your message to an audience.

How to be more productive

Sometimes it's challenging to bring a project to a conclusion. We procrastinate, become side-tracked, or look for excuses. The project gets fuzzier, rather than sharper, the longer we work.

Lock yourself into a situation where you have no choice but to bring things to a conclusion.

Two rock musicians were locked in a room in 1962 and told they couldn't come out until they'd written a hit song. No song, no freedom. Their captor was their manager, and the occasion became rock legend. The two musicians' rock band was good at cover versions, but their manager realized the only way to be popular and unique was through writing their own songs. They made a first attempt, but they didn't have a method. Time passed, nothing emerged, so they hummed and strummed, trying everything. A night passed. Finally, they emerged in the morning with a song. Not the hard rock song everyone expected but a ballad with the lyrics, 'All I hear is the sound, of rain falling on the ground, I sit and watch, as tears go by.'

The writing duo was Mick Jagger and Keith Richards of the Rolling Stones. Richards explained: 'So what Andrew Oldham did was lock us up in the kitchen for a night and say, "Don't come out without a song." We sat around and came up with "As Tears Go By". Jagger and Richards both credit their manager as the catalyst for their songwriting collaboration.

In the 80s I was commissioned to do a portrait of Mick Jagger, for the cover of a Rolling Stones biography. There was a deadline of only a week, but it helped me to focus. I grew up listening to the Stones' music and it was important to me to be satisfied with Jagger's portrait. If I'd had a long time, I could have overthought the task. I shut myself away and worked quickly until I'd finished. 'A deadline is negative inspiration. Still, it's better than no inspiration at all,' said feminist writer Rita Mae Brown.

1   Make a commitment that forces you to get your creative act together. Get a deadline from a publisher, gallery or record company – something to galvanize you into doing what you want.

2   It's a myth that creativity thrives when you're free. The creative are often under pressure to deliver. When there is a deadline, the human mind becomes focused. Samuel Johnson pointed out, 'When a man knows he is to be hanged in a fortnight, it concentrates his mind wonderfully.' Give your work your full attention. Some things are beyond our control, so the things we can control deserve our full attention because we can affect the result.

Break free from yourself

Sometimes we are defined by our past. People judge us on a past version of ourselves, and it's a trap that's important to escape. If your history defines you as someone you no longer are, you must reinvent yourself.

Maria Gurwik-Górska arrived in Paris during the 1920s, a penniless immigrant. She had been born into a wealthy, close Polish family, but lived in Russia and the Revolution stripped her of everything. She used her impoverished situation as an opportunity to shed her past and reboot. She had a fresh vision of herself as an artist, a problematic occupation for a woman in that era. She determined to create the paintings she wanted and to earn a living from them. Her paintings were a curious mix of traditional Russian realist paintings and cubism.

She established a reputation in Paris galleries as an ingenious self-promoter with talent and a bubbly personality. She changed her name to Tamara de Lempicka and reinvented herself as a new kind of modern woman – a self-styled, free-thinking, jazz-age femme fatale. In 1925 she painted an astounding twenty-eight new works in six months for her first solo exhibition.

Lempicka threw off all the traditions and expectations holding her back. She didn't become fiction but revealed her true self. Her message was clear and direct – she was unashamed to be a strong woman with clear ambitions. She defined herself through her look, beliefs, and going all out for what she wanted. With a clear core idea of yourself, you can be whoever you want. Diverse figures from fashion designers Karl Lagerfeld and Louis Vuitton to Lady Gaga and Madonna – who is an avid collector of Lempicka's paintings – have all acknowledged that Lempicka's attitude of reinvention inspired them.

Like Lempicka, Katheryn Hudson led a constricted, regulated childhood. Her parents were born-again Christians and pastors who strictly adhered to their religious values. Katheryn and her family even demonstrated against Madonna outside her concerts.

Katheryn became a gospel singer in her late teens and released a debut LP in 2001. It sold 200 copies, so she got a day job and sang at open mike nights in bars and clubs in the evenings.

It's natural to want your parents to be proud of you. Our parents want the best for us, but sometimes their vision of who we should be is different from our own. Katheryn realized she wasn't being her true, authentic self and had the inner strength to transform. She moved to Los Angeles, changed her name, and developed a new, larger than life character that was an exaggeration of her real self. She wrote songs to reflect her strong, independent spirit and sang about taboo subjects. Her first single as Katy Perry was 'I Kissed a Girl'. It went to number one in the *Billboard* Hot 100 in 2008.

Katy Perry told the *Guardian* newspaper, 'I didn't want to be Katheryn Hudson. I hated that, it was too scary for me, so I decided to be someone else.' To stand up for yourself, you have to develop a rebellious spirit, strength and determination. Perry had strength of character and a refusal to give up on herself.

Katy Perry's record sales stand at over 150 million. When she performed at the Super Bowl half-time show in 2015, she pulled in the highest ever audience with 118 million people tuning in, more than for the game itself. At one of her concerts, her father looked at the adulation of her thousands of fans, and said, 'They're loving and worshipping the wrong thing.'

1   Work out who you are and what you want to achieve. Most people are too lazy to look deeply into themselves and gain a deep understanding. Are you your true self?

2   If not, what is preventing you from being your true self? It could be pressures from family and friends, or practical matters like where you live. Move from the false version of yourself to the correct version. Sometimes we're forced to reinvent ourselves when a business fails; we're made redundant, suffer grief, start a new relationship, or move to a new home. A traumatic event forces you to become a new version of yourself. Many years ago, I stood in for a university lecturer who was taking maternity leave. It was the first time I'd taught, and I immediately found I had to take control of the studio, or the students talked over me. I took on a new role and brought out a hidden side of my personality. What do you need to let go of to achieve success?

3   How will you overcome these obstacles preventing you from being what you want? Learning new skills will help you become the person you want to be. Lempicka learned how to paint; it was what she had always wanted to do. Like her, you could reach your full potential and enable yourself to pursue your ambitions with renewed zest. Learning motivates you and introduces you to different people and ideas. If you go through a significant change in your circumstances, you must discover new ways to think and act.

Use your strengths

We have skills and talents in one area of our life and we don't realize we could use them in another. Or, we're so used to our talents that we forget about them.

It's important to be aware of all your strengths and look for opportunities to use them. Most careers have unplanned twists and turns. People change industries and spheres, and life often throws us unexpected opportunities. In a rapidly changing world, you need to be able to adapt your abilities quickly to new situations. Skills from one area can be transferred to another and achieve astonishing results.

During the Second World War, the Nazis feared the US Army's 23rd Headquarters Special Troops. The Germans' equipment was old and often broke down, while photos from reconnaissance planes showed the 23rd had 600 brand new tanks and a huge amount of artillery. Nonetheless, as the war reached its endgame in March 1945, the Nazis went to launch a major attack on the 23rd at the River Rhine.

But the 23rd had vanished. To move tanks and artillery takes hours, but they had disappeared. It was impossible. The Nazis had been drawn into a trap. The US 9th Army had secretly surrounded them, and now they attacked. There was little German resistance and the battle ended swiftly with few casualties on either side.

The vanishing act of the 23rd was one of the most astonishing battle strategies in history. How they did it has lessons for us all.

Strength is an illusion

The soldiers of the 23rd were artists, actors, designers, architects and musicians that had been recruited from advertising agencies, communications companies and art schools such as the Pratt Institute in New York. The artists of the 23rd were given conventional army training and could fight like any other soldiers. But their real skill was their training as artists, and it proved to be more useful on the battlefield than their training as soldiers. More than that, it gave them a unique advantage. These soldiers were crucial to bringing new creative ideas to the battlefield.

One of these soldiers was the abstract artist Ellsworth Kelly, whose training at art college had given him a deep understanding of vision. A painting is a two-dimensional image creating an illusion of three dimensions, and Kelly used his knowledge of illusion in warfare. He and the other artists of the 23rd stopped designing camouflage to hide US tanks. Instead, they made American tanks clearly visible to the Germans – fake inflatable tanks. They created fake vehicles and troop encampments to deceive the enemy reconnaissance aircraft; their weapons were rubber and imagination. The tanks were exactly the same size as real tanks and were painted convincingly. Once the tanks had served their purpose, the 23rd deflated them and simply melted away, leaving the Nazis stranded. General Simpson, the commander of the 9th Army, said the deception could have saved the lives of 10,000 men.

Kelly understood vision and used it in a way no conventional soldier would. We understand the world by observing, but seeing is not passive because vision takes place in our brain rather than in our eyes. Information about colour, shape and movement floods into our eyes and is processed by our brain. The neuroscientist David Marr explained that vision 'is a process that produces from images of the external world a description that is useful to the viewer and not cluttered with irrelevant information'. Everything we see is converted to a simplified understanding in our minds; research reveals that our brain would need to be larger than a house to handle everything seen by our eyes, so it selects the most plausible interpretation of what we see.

Kelly used his understanding of illusion in an unfamiliar field, and in the contemporary world we also need to be able to cope with unfamiliar situations. Adopt a flexible mindset. Don't think of yourself as someone with fixed abilities. 'I initially moved to San Francisco to become a research associate for one of the top young heart surgeons in the country. Everything I learned in that position showed me that skills, talent and expertise are transferable,' said Chris Gardner, clinical researcher and businessman. Identify your skills and abilities and then work out how you can use them in a new area.

1   Be adaptable. Think of ways to transfer skills from one area of your life to another. Identify your 'hard' skills and abilities (a knowledge of computer programs, ability to speak a foreign language or technical skills), then work out how you can use them in a different sphere.

2   Identify your 'soft skills' (such as people skills, creative thinking and problem-solving – more difficult to define and explain, but equally useful) and figure out how to apply them to a new situation.

3   Sometimes we're so busy working, our real strengths get lost in the hectic schedule. Identify your core skills and strengths. Then work out how to apply them.

Become a firestarter

'Firestarter' is a term used in the arts to describe someone motivated and inspired. They search inside themselves and find their authentic voice; consequently, their belief and purpose spread like a fire. They ignite change in their field because they maintain their core belief no matter who pours cold water.

In the 1570s, the Roman Catholic Church had strict guidelines for painting biblical scenes. Religious figures had to exude serenity and perfection. Break their rules, and you'd answer to the all-powerful Roman Catholic Inquisition.

The Renaissance Italian painter Paolo Veronese's enormous painting *The Last Supper* broke the Inquisition's instructions. He did not show Christ as a stiff, stylized religious icon, but placed him in an everyday setting – a lively dinner party. The disciples were there with jesters, cats and dogs, living lives the man on the street could relate to and understand.

The Roman Catholic Inquisition accused Veronese of heresy, an offence punishable by death, and summoned him to the Sacred Court in Venice. The Inquisition struck fear into the population's hearts by torturing, imprisoning or publicly burning heretics, and Veronese's life hung in the balance.

In front of the Inquisition, even prominent noblemen pleaded for leniency. The Inquisition projected its power and authority as its members sat on lavishly ornamented thrones in a vast hall, with classical columns swathed in gold leaf. They wore thick velvet robes lined with silk, and ostentatious gold rings with church insignia. By contrast, Veronese struck a humble, powerless figure when he stood before them. The Inquisition demanded an explanation for every detail of the painting, and Veronese was surprisingly bold. He didn't cower or apologize like previous defendants. Painting was not a job to him but something that filled him with conviction and a higher purpose. He believed in the message in his work and stood up for it. The onlookers feared they would burn him alive.

When the Inquisition ordered Veronese to change the painting, there were two certainties: the Inquisition would not compromise, and neither would Veronese. He wouldn't ruin a masterpiece. Veronese made none of the changes demanded, but instead found a way out: he changed the title from *The Last Supper* to *The Feast in the House of Levi*, a Bible story about a party full of sinners. The change of title meant that the Inquisition could no longer accuse him of heresy. Veronese did what we should all be doing in the face of such situations and refused to follow a small, stupid rule. He knew the more profound message of his painting would connect with people, and he stood up to the Inquisition and won. Veronese saved an artwork that hundreds of thousands still flock to see at the Galleria dell'Accademia in Venice. In fact, Veronese was the opposite of a heretic; he was a devout Catholic with a deep understanding of the Bible and he wanted to communicate it truthfully.

Artists in the Renaissance were not lone individuals but small businesses, comparable to a small film company or start-up today. Veronese ran a large studio with many employees who depended on him for their livelihoods. Imagine Veronese as a small start-up and the Inquisition as a global corporation. Like many big corporations, they had lost touch with their real purpose and were only concerned with maintaining their dominance. Small, authentic companies can stay true to their core aims. When people in the arts, like Veronese, publicly confronted the Inquisition, it was the beginning of the end.

My wife and I often visit the Church of Saint Sebastian in Venice, where Veronese spent decades working on the paintings, ceiling canvases and frescoes on the nave and altar walls. The church is full of visitors from around the world and I doubt if many are Christian, yet Veronese's work speaks to them. The stories of his artworks are uplifting ones we can all relate to. Veronese knew why he painted, and that gave him integrity and inner strength. It also gave his work a lasting brilliance that still inspires.

1   Determine what your core beliefs are and stay true to them. They are the rock to build on.

2   What do you want to change? 'Firestarter' is the term for innovators who spearhead change. They break the rules and start the fire, not for its own sake but with a purpose. The negativity of others does not dampen a firestarter's spirits. They instigate change and make the world a more creative and exciting place.

3 Anyone can be a firestarter with the right motivation and attitude. The firestarter's drive to produce brilliant work ensures they break away from the pack. Creating something new is hard and takes guts and inner strength.

Overcome fear of failure

Psychologists believe we use 'avoidance behaviours' to control our fear of failure. Because we set goals we can achieve and avoid those we might fail to achieve, we reduce our insecurity in the short term but increase it in the long term. When we avoid stretching ourselves with lofty ambitions, we fail to live up to our true potential. Reasonable goals don't fire up your enthusiasm, so you put less effort into them. If the reward is mediocre, you don't try as hard.

Steve Sasson and his wife were in Yellowstone National Park on their summer holiday in the late 1990s. They stood alongside hundreds of other tourists and watched the geyser known as Old Faithful burst into the air. Sasson looked around and whispered to his wife, 'It's happening.' 'What?' she asked. Watching the tourists, the quiet, unassuming Sasson saw the revolution he'd instigated that had transformed society like the Gutenberg press or the telephone.

In 1973, Sasson had been working for the photography technology company Kodak, but he'd had a problem we all face from time to time – he felt his work was mediocre and uninspiring. He was an overlooked minor employee working on low-priority side projects in a remote lab at the back of the building. Kodak was one of the world's wealthiest companies, but although they invested in innovation, they had become prosperous and self-satisfied, taking little interest in developing new ideas.

Left to his own devices, Sasson didn't write reports on his project's development and rarely saw his supervisor. However, he made an extraordinary decision and set himself an unreasonable goal – to produce a camera with no mechanical moving parts. Sasson put tremendous pressure on himself and took advantage of his lowly, overlooked position. He said later, 'For a scientist it was the perfect situation. Freedom to experiment, no particular goal, and no one was paying attention.'

In 1975 he emerged from obscurity and proudly presented a revolutionary device to the Kodak executives. They sat back in soft leather chairs at a long oak table in a luxurious conference room as he revealed a gadget the size of a toaster. It took a photo of everyone in the room, and almost instantly, an image popped up on a screen. He had made history – the first digital camera. It was virtually identical to today's models, with compressed JPEG images and a memory card. The image quality was low, but it was a prototype, and the resolution could be improved. He excitedly explained how he could send images over a telephone line (the internet was not invented until over a decade later).

Kodak was a business anchored in selling film cameras, film and film processing, but the digital camera required no film, photographic paper, or processing. No one was shouting, 'We need a digital camera.' Psychologists call this idea Einstellung – we stick to what we know and what is familiar. The Kodak executives made a rational judgment and stamped on the invention. Why give the public something they hadn't demanded? It took Sony and other camera-makers without

Kodak's long tradition with film to see its potential, while in 2012, Kodak filed for bankruptcy.

At Yellowstone Park, when he saw the tourists taking photos on digital cameras, Sasson realized his invention was becoming ubiquitous. Personal computers enabled the downloading of images and digital cameras democratized the expensive art of photography. A while ago, photographers were an exclusive elite; now, we're all photographers with phones capable of taking high-quality images and immediately sharing them with the world.

If Henry Ford had arranged focus groups, they would have asked for improvements to the horse and carriage – not a motor car. During an interview with *Fortune* magazine, Steve Jobs commented, 'In most people's vocabularies, design means veneer. It's the fabric of the curtains or sofa. But to me, nothing could be further from the meaning of design.' He went on to say, 'That doesn't mean we don't listen to customers, but it's hard for them to tell you what they want when they've never seen anything remotely like it before.'

President Obama awarded Sasson the 2009 US National Medal of Technology and Innovation. The ceremony at the White House was a formal event, but as Obama placed the medal around Sasson's neck, hundreds of digital cameras clicked.

1 Be aware of your 'avoidance behaviours'. What are you avoiding because of fear of failure? Is a fear of failure leading you to safe, attainable goals? 'We're a pretty strong bunch, and we have pretty lofty goals,' said Megan Rapinoe, captain of the World Cup-winning US soccer team.

2   Set yourself an unreasonable goal. The pressure from society is to set reasonable goals so you don't fail, but safe goals equal safe achievements. People who achieve the extraordinary set goals beyond their limitations – goals their colleagues and friends thought were impossible and ridiculous. It's counterintuitive, but it's easier to achieve huge goals because everyone else aims at the small ones. Trying to attain what seems unattainable forces you to think differently. If the goal is extraordinary, the achievement will be too.

Explore broadly

Whatever field you work in, there is pressure to produce the finished product as soon as possible. It seems reasonable to want the solution quickly in order to save time and money, yet focusing on the answer is a mistake.

Mir Imran is an Indian inventor and medical entrepreneur who has produced astonishing results with a counterintuitive method. When he was a child, his mother despaired – her son destroyed every toy she bought him, especially anything mechanical, and she worried what the future held for such a destructive child. But Imran wasn't destructive – he was just curious about how things worked. And as an adult, this curiosity led him to an extraordinarily successful working method; after only three years of studying bioengineering at Rutgers Medical School in New Jersey, he attained nearly 200 patents for medical devices he'd invented. He went on to create hundreds of others. Millions of patients would have died if he hadn't developed an implantable cardiac defibrillator to restore a racing heart to its normal rhythm. Millions more owe their lives to his ablation catheter for cardiac arrhythmias.

Imran's medical technology career started in the late 1970s when a school for children with cerebral palsy was looking for an engineer to develop communication aides for quadriplegic children. Although still an undergraduate at Rutgers University, Imran tried to help. He met a six-year-old girl who had such severe cerebral palsy that she couldn't control her hands or legs or communicate at all. Imran created a customized machine to connect with the few muscles she had voluntary control over, and suddenly she could communicate. The machine had a powerful impact on her, but also on Imran. It sparked a lifelong interest in clinical research. Imran was struck by how many unsolved medical problems existed, and worked sixteen-hour days to devise solutions. He didn't use the standard research methods but developed his technique to produce innovation. A lesson to us all: develop your unique research methods, whatever your field.

Imran was uneasy at medical school. As he explained, 'Everything I studied was rote memorization; very few things really had explanations.' He felt you needed a deep understanding of a problem in order to solve it; your task was to find out as much as possible.

Research takes time and curiosity, but people often want to cut corners and get straight to the solution. 'Innovation is the process of defining the problem and understanding the problem – not solving it,' Imran said.

An agency commissioned to produce a TV advert for a brand of butter once asked me to help. They couldn't think of an idea even though they had researched everything to do with butter and had even seen it in production. I set a series of tasks for them to explore the product in greater depth, including persuading them to visit a margarine factory. They were horrified at the number of chemicals poured into margarine, which led them to the idea that they could promote butter's natural qualities. Their successful idea came directly from this research.

Imran's method was to develop a thorough understanding of a subject, 'and then the solution will emerge from that understanding'. Setting out to solve the problem is a mistake because your search is narrow – it's better to explore broadly. You need to understand everything about your task, even if 99 per cent of the information becomes useless. Explore every aspect of your problem deeply. The solution presents itself from asking questions.

1   Once you've established the obvious things to explore, actively search for the least obvious. Look for details others have missed and delve deeply.

2   Develop 'a rage to master', which Boston College psychologist Ellen Winner identified as a key component of curiosity. It's a desperate need to explore and to know everything about your chosen field. 'I am just a child who has never grown up. I still keep asking these "how" and "why" questions. Occasionally, I find an answer,' said Stephen Hawking in *A Brief History of Time*.

3   Resist the pressure to get instant results. Enjoy exploring your subject for the joy of exploration.

Adopt a new perspective

We all fall into the trap of doing the same things in the same way, but the same old thinking gets the same old results. Psychiatrists term this 'repetition compulsion'. It's comfortable to do the same things in the same way. To break the pattern, people and organizations have to adopt new perspectives.

When Dale Chihuly drove down a road in England in 1979, he experienced the first of two incidents that transformed him from a mediocre professional into a revolutionary hailed as the most radical thinker in his field. Chihuly worked within the traditional standards of his profession, but these incidents forced him to break free.

The first incident occurred when the car he was travelling in smashed head-on into another vehicle at high speed. He

wasn't wearing a seat belt and he flew through the windscreen. His face required 250 stitches, and he lost the sight in one eye. It would be traumatic for anyone, but it was catastrophic for Chihuly because he was a glass-blower. The standard practice was to judge vases and bowls on their symmetry. With only one eye, he could no longer see in three dimensions and assess symmetry. He ran a business with employees who depended on his skills, so he urgently needed a solution.

The second incident, which provided the answer, happened when he was bodyboarding in the sea. He dislocated his shoulder so severely that it was left permanently weak. I've tried glass-blowing on the island of Murano in Venice. A glass factory is like a fairground in hell where furnaces blast out heat and roar like volcanoes, and glass-blowing is a strenuous physical activity requiring extraordinary physical endurance; one piece can take hours of hard physical labour.

Chihuly's craft required perfect eyesight to judge symmetry, and the strength and stamina to hold a massive metal rod for

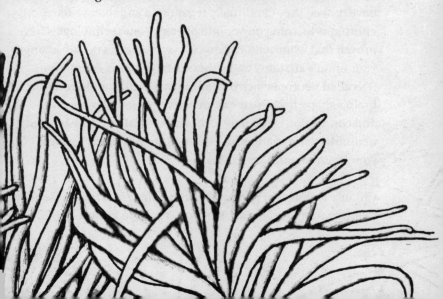

hours a day, so the loss of an eye and his physical strength forced him to step back and direct his assistants. The trouble was, his assistants didn't have his skill level, but because his business was moderately successful many people depended on him for their livelihoods. Chihuly needed a new approach, so he allowed them to abandon symmetry and let the molten glass fall naturally into swirls. Asymmetry became the groundbreaking feature of his hanging glass sculptures. I regularly stand awestruck under one of his works at the Victoria & Albert Museum in London – a gigantic explosion of iridescent blue, green and yellow glass hanging from the ceiling. Thousands of hand-blown elements teem with a luminous mass of vivid colours, like a giant anemone with writhing tentacles shooting out squiggles of fluid colour. The switch to being a director rather than a hands-on maker enabled him to create massive works, tens of feet in dimension, rather than reasonably sized vases for coffee tables.

It's a myth that our brains become more and more solid over our lifetime like slowly setting concrete; neuroscientists have proved they continually regenerate and that we have enormous learning power into old age. New technologies have proven that whoever and however old you are, you can change your brain's anatomy and structure by thinking creatively. It's called neuroplasticity. Reading this book has altered your brain's shape because it has created new neural pathways and connections. You may feel as if perception is passive, but neuroplasticity enables new thoughts to physically reshape your brain's neural structures.

Chihuly's change in perspective catapulted him from obscurity to international attention. His studio grew to hundreds of employees, and his works sold for massive amounts. He had breathed life into the glass-blowing world, no longer viewed as a craft because his works were elevated to the status of art and exhibited in galleries and museums.

To transform your career with a fresh perspective, you don't need a car accident. Perry Chen's transformation was as spectacular as Chihuly's, but it was the result of his own decision-making. He was CEO of Kickstarter but changed his role to chairman. It altered his perspective; no longer engrossed in day-to-day chores, he was able to speculate on the company's long-term future.

As an American global crowdfunding platform specializing in bringing creative projects to life, Kickstarter received billions of dollars of pledges from millions of backers to fund hundreds of thousands of films, stage shows, comics and video games. But like Chihuly, Chen changed his perspective by stepping back. He asked big questions about the deeper purpose of the company, and he and co-founder Yancey Strickler made a unique decision. Instead of becoming a public company, in 2015, they converted to a Public Benefit Corporation (PBC) and resolved never to sell the company or launch it on the stock market. The mantra in Silicon Valley was to grow quickly and sell out fast. Becoming a PBC meant they were no longer legally compelled to focus on maximizing profits. They could make the welfare of their employees their priority instead.

1   Are you suffering from 'repetition compulsion'? Are you doing the same old things in the same old way because it's easier than thinking up new, better approaches? 'I feel confident imposing change on myself. It's a lot more fun progressing than looking back. That's why I need to throw curve balls,' said David Bowie.

2   What accepted standards are holding you back? Step back and see your life and work from a bigger perspective. 'Change the way you look at things and the things you look at change,' said the bestselling author Wayne W. Dyer. Accepting the standards of your profession limits your thinking. Chihuly had to give up skills that were precious to him and that he'd developed over the years, but as he explained, 'Once I stepped back, I liked the view.' What accepted standards are holding you back?

Make a breakthrough

It's easier to take the safe, secure choices in life, but you won't learn anything. A breakthrough creative act needs an investment of time with no guarantee of success. Stretch yourself and attempt an unreasonably huge task and you'll find your true capabilities.

Théodore Géricault was a twenty-seven-year-old painter in the early nineteenth century. He was frustrated because he worked hard but went unnoticed. He was producing good paintings but so were his rivals, so he decided to create a breakthrough work to stand out from the crowd. He had limited finances so he used his only resources – time and an innovative mind. He devoted his every waking moment over the months that followed to one gigantic painting, and used five strategies to make it a breakthrough work:

∗ **Controversy:** Géricault was deliberately controversial. He intended to submit his painting to the annual exhibition of the stuffy and conservative Paris Salon, the most prestigious event in the art world, and he chose to paint a notorious contemporary event to cause uproar. The *Medusa*, a French Navy frigate, had foundered. The crew had built a raft but only ten survived, being tossed around by huge waves for thirteen days. Their accounts in the newspapers revealed shocking brutality and cannibalism and Géricault portrayed the full horror of the disaster, deliberately setting out to offend the bourgeois Paris audience.

The painting, *The Raft of the Medusa* (1819), showed a moment when survivors on the raft signalled to a distant rescue ship. Their desperation was graphically depicted – an old man held his dead son while another pulled his hair in exasperation and corpses in the foreground slipped into the waves. The only black survivor frantically waved a shirt to attract the ship – putting a black man centre stage was shocking for the time.

* **Scale:** Géricault realized scale would create impact, so he made his painting a monumental twenty-four feet wide, as big as a cinema screen, so the viewer felt they were completely immersed in the scene.

* **Risk:** Géricault devoted himself entirely to the painting. Like any creative person, he put an enormous investment of time and effort into a huge risk. To gamble everything on one painting was like putting eighteen months' salary on one spin of the roulette wheel. He shaved his head, and split up with his lover because he couldn't spare the time. He slept in his studio, had his meals delivered and only went outside to research. He built a life-size replica of the raft in his studio and hired the carpenter who had built the original to ensure authenticity. He used three survivors as models and painted them from life. Many of the figures were life-size and spilled into the foreground, making the viewer feel they were being physically sucked into the action. It was the nineteenth-century equivalent of an apocalyptic movie.

* **Research:** Géricault spent months painstakingly researching before he started to paint. He interviewed two survivors – Henri Savigny, a surgeon, and Alexandre

Corréard, an engineer, and their horrific accounts inspired the frenetic power of the painting. He was obsessed with accurately depicting the flesh tones of corpses and spent hours sketching bodies in the morgue and the faces of dying patients in hospitals. He sailed on ships to study the weather and filled his sketchbooks with seascapes, waves and clouds.

* **Distinctiveness:** Géricault made his painting distinctive from all the other work around it by painting in a highly dramatic style. It was the complete opposite of the detached, cool and accurate neoclassical style of the time.

When *The Raft of the Medusa* was shown at the 1819 Paris Salon, it won a gold medal and Géricault was awarded the honour of a commission from the Salon. Yet because it was aggressively political and artistically confrontational, many critics were negative. Although the painting eventually became an icon of French romanticism, there was a problem: that movement hadn't yet started. Gallery visitors didn't say, 'Wow, the first French romantic painting – he's taking painting in a new direction!' They said, 'That's a terrible neoclassical painting – he's not keeping to the rules!' But the controversy added to Géricault's reputation; he had achieved his breakthrough and he had the attention of the art world and the public. He had worked out what he had to do to make a breakthrough and had made all the necessary sacrifices. More importantly, he had cultivated the ability to keep going when his mind and body wanted to stop.

The Louvre Museum in Paris bought *The Raft of the Medusa* and it has long been one of their main attractions. The painting has since influenced many notable artists, including

Delacroix (who modelled for one of the figures), Turner, Corbet and Manet.

Do the thing you ought not to do

Mark Twain explained, 'The best swordsman in the world doesn't need to fear the second-best swordsman in the world; no, the person for him to be afraid of is some ignorant antagonist who has never had a sword in his hand before; he doesn't do the thing he ought to do, and so the expert isn't prepared for him; he does the thing he ought not to do; and often it catches the expert out and ends him on the spot.'

Do the thing you ought not to do, and you enter a world of discovery.

In 1960, the writer Roald Dahl's son Theo was hit by a New York taxi and developed hydrocephalus, a condition in which fluid accumulates in the skull and makes the patient's head swell. A Holter shunt drained the excess liquid from Theo's brain, but the tubes kept clogging, causing him pain and possible brain damage.

All over the world, hundreds of people experienced traumatic pain because no one had produced a clog-proof device. The medical profession simply had to use the equipment supplied. Medicine was not Dahl's field, which gave him an outsider's perspective. He determined to invent something better, so he sketched an idea for a new device on the back of a newspaper and showed it to his son's neurosurgeon, Kenneth Till.

Dahl's hobby was flying model aircraft, and he transplanted his knowledge of miniature hydraulic pumps (used in the undercarriages of model aircraft) from one field into another. Dahl spent months scribbling calculations, building prototypes, and testing the pressure in the valves. Together with Till and his friend Stanley Wade, Dahl developed a new, more robust mechanism that was easy to sterilize and didn't clog. They patented the invention and agreed never to accept any profit from it. As a result, thousands of people have benefitted from the Wade-Dahl-Till valve.

Successful creative people often come from outside their field of success because they bring a fresh perspective. The existing doctrines and assumptions do not bind them. Because they don't know what is reasonable, they have no fear of doing what's unreasonable. 'I became a scriptwriter with absolutely no idea of how to write a script whatsoever. I still feel a bit of an outsider in that regard. If I can maintain that approach to screenwriting, it will continue to be enjoyable,' said singer Nick Cave.

Tremendous innovation occurs when someone from a different field reframes the problem. By reframing it, they unlock the solution. For Dahl, a complete lack of medical knowledge did not deter him, and this was the key to creating complex equipment.

A physician called Professor Kevin Moore at the Royal Free Hospital in London read my book *The Art of Creative Thinking* and asked me into the Royal Free to deliver workshops to his Applied Medical Science students.

Medicine increasingly requires problem-solvers, so Kevin Moore had set them a real project. A new drug was of enormous benefit to patients with severe liver problems. It dissolved the fatty tissue developing around an unfit liver and prevented the need for serious intervention such as an operation or liver transplant. But patients kept forgetting to take the drugs at a specific time, which made them ineffective. I suggested trying a design technique called gamification – introducing game-playing into an area you wouldn't expect. The students developed an app to make taking the drug on time into a game. The patients scored points for taking their medication on the dot, and they could link to each other to join a competition to get the highest score. Suddenly taking the pills at the right time became engaging.

1   Don't do the thing you ought to. You can overcome a lack of technical skill with help from others.

2   Ask someone from a different field to comment on what you're doing. They'll notice problems you've overlooked.

3   Don't let other people's thinking become your thinking. Developing an independent mindset is about starting with a fresh attitude every day.

Acknowledgements

I would like to thank Zelda Malan, Louis Judkins and Scarlet Judkins for their advice and help during the creation of this book – and also for being models for many of the illustrations. I'd like to thank my agent, Jonathan Conway, for his input into its development from its early stages through to its conclusion. Thanks to my editor, Matthew Cole, for believing in *Make Brilliant Work*, and for his insights and advice; I'm also very grateful to my copy editor, Amber Burlinson, for her painstaking work. My colleagues and students in the universities where I teach have been a valuable source of inspiration.

Bibliography and references

Addison, John, '7 Ways to Go From Ordinary to Extraordinary', *SUCCESS* (22 May 2017) https://www.success.com/7-ways-to-go-from-ordinary-to-extraordinary/

Adjaye, David, *Adjaye · Africa · Architecture*, Thames & Hudson (2016)

Al, Stephan, 'How Robert Venturi Helped Turn Las Vegas Into America's Architecture', *Garage* (26 November 2018) https://garage.vice.com/en_us/article/zm548j/how-robert-venturi-helped-turn-las-vegas-into-americas-architecture

Alexander, Alma, '"Dick and Jane" vs Dr. Seuss', *almaalexander* (21 September 2015) http://www.almaalexander.org/dick-and-jane-vs-dr-seuss/

Alifano, Roberto, *Twenty-Four Conversations with Borges: Interviews by Roberto Alifano 1981–1983*, Grove/Atlantic (1984)

Allen, Greg, 'Blowing Up Tanks: Ellsworth Kelly and the Camouflage Secret Army', *greg.org* (14 October 2011) http://greg.org/archive/2011/10/14/blowing_up_tanks_ellsworth_kelly_and_the_camouflage_secret_army.html

Amed, Imran, 'Reinventing Gucci', *Business of Fashion* (22 September 2015) https://www.businessoffashion.com/articles/ceo-talk/reinventing-gucci

Anderson, Chris, 'Elon Musk's Mission to Mars', *Wired* (21 October 2012) https://www.wired.com/2012/10/ff-elon-musk-qa/

Artble, 'Caravaggio Style and Technique' http://www.artble.com/artists/caravaggio/more_information/style_and_technique

Art Quotes, 'Janine Parsons Quotes' http://www.art-quotes.com/auth_search.php?authid=5433#.YDzRkun7SRs

Art Quotes, 'Hans Richter Quotes' http://www.art-quotes.com/auth_search.php?authid=3048#.YEIoYJOeRGM

Augustyn, Heather, 'Speaking in Pastiche: Lee "Scratch" Perry and Subatomic Sound System Revisit "Super Ape"', *PopMatters* (10 November 2017) https://www.popmatters.com/lee-scratch-perry-2507902220.html

Axelrod, Maura, *Maurizio Cattelan: Be Right Back* (2016) https://vimeo.com/205525246

Azerrad, Michael, *Come As You Are: The Story of Nirvana*, Virgin Books (1993)

Ballard, J. G., *Miracles of Life*, HarperCollins (2008)

Beckett, Andy, 'Arts: A Strange Case', *Independent* (23 October 2011) https://www.independent.co.uk/arts-entertainment/arts-a-strange-case-1581580.html

Benedictus, Leo, 'Brian Duffy: "Photography was dead by 1972"', *Guardian* (12 January 2010) https://www.theguardian.com/artanddesign/2010/jan/12/brian-duffy

Bernstein, Jeremy, 'King of the Quantum', *New York Review* (26 September 1991) https://www.nybooks.com/articles/1991/09/26/king-of-the-quantum/

Biography.com, 'Henri Matisse Biography' (16 August 2019) https://www.biography.com/artist/henri-matisse

Biskind, Peter, *Easy Riders, Raging Bulls*, Simon & Schuster (1998)

Brassaï, *Conversations with Picasso*, University of Chicago Press (1999)

Bronson, Po, 'HotMale', *Wired* (1 December 1998) https://www.wired.com/1998/12/hotmale/

Bronson, Po, 'What's the Big Idea?', *Stanford Magazine* (September/October 1999) https://stanfordmag.org/contents/what-s-the-big-idea

Bruni, Frank, 'How Alessandro Michele Made Gucci Relevant Again', *Sydney Morning Herald* (1 December 2018) https://www.smh.com.au/lifestyle/fashion/how-alessandro-michele-made-gucci-relevant-again-20181126-p50id1.html

Buntz, Brian, 'Mir Imran: An Innovator's Journey', *Medical Device and Diagnostic Industry* (4 June 2012) http://www.mddionline.com/article/mir-imran-innovator's-journey

Cambers, Dahlia S., 'The Law of Averages 1: Normman and Norma', *Cabinet Magazine* (Fall 2004) http://www.cabinetmagazine.org/issues/15/cambers.php

Carney, Ray, *Cassavetes on Cassavetes*, Faber and Faber (2001)

Carney, Ray, The Films of John Cassavetes: Pragmatism, Modernism, and the Movies, Cambridge University Press, (1994)

Cinemorgue Wiki, '*Apocalypse Now*, Fandom' https://cinemorgue.fandom.com/wiki/Apocalypse_Now_(1979)

Cohen, Jesse, 'Science Friction', *Los Angeles Times* (13 July 2008)

Cookson, Guy, 'From a Boring Factory to a Squeezed Lemon: A Brief History of Alessi', *Hotfoot* (14 November 2017) https://www.hotfootdesign.co.uk/white-space/brief-history-alessi/

Cragg, Michael, '"I created this character called Katy Perry. I didn't want to be Katheryn Hudson. It was too scary"', *Observer* (11 June 2017) https://www.theguardian.com/music/2017/jun/11/katy-perry-interview-witness-album-glastonbury

Croteau, Jeanne, 'The Stunning Transformation of Katy Perry', *The List* (26 July 2017) https://www.thelist.com/71890/stunning-transformation-katy-perry/?utm_campaign=clip

Delli Santi, Angela, 'The Innovator – Mir A. Imran', *Rutgers Magazine* http://soe.rutgers.edu/story/innovator-mir-imran

Dowling, Dan, 'How Ordinary People Become Extraordinary', *Entrepreneur* (3 April 2018) https://www.entrepreneur.com/article/310605

Duchscher, Towani, 'Flight of Transcendence: Exploring Flight as a Metaphor for Transcendent Teaching and Learning', University of Calgary (2015)

Durham University, 'Call for Counterintuitive Ideas' https://www.dur.ac.uk/chi/ideas/call/

English, Tom and Wilma, 'Wrongly Rejected (Encouragement for Creators)', *Angel at the Door* (22 July 2016) https://www.angelatthedoor.com/2016/07/

Entrepreneur staff, '6 Entrepreneurs Share the Brilliant, Crazy Ways They Took Their Companies from Pennies to Profit', *Entrepreneur* (18 May 2018) https://www.entrepreneur.com/article/311861

Estrin, James, 'Kodak's First Digital Moment', *New York Times* (12 August 2015) https://lens.blogs.nytimes.com/2015/08/12/kodaks-first-digital-moment/

Etherington, Rose, 'Lou Ruvo Centre for Brain Health by Frank Gehry', *Dezeen* (17 June 2010) https://www.dezeen.com/2010/06/17/lou-ruvo-center-for-brain-health-by-frank-gehry/

Evening Standard, 'Con Artist? Critics Dismissed Picasso Too, Says Damien Hirst', *Evening Standard* (2 April 2012) https://www.standard.co.uk/go/london/exhibitions/con-artist-critics-dismissed-picasso-too-says-damien-hirst-7608408.html

Farnam Street, 'How to Think: The Skill You've Never Been Taught', *Farnam Street blog* https://fs.blog/2015/08/how-to-think/

Flaherty, Joseph, '50 Big Companies that Started with Little or No Money', *Hackernoon* (20 March 2018) https://hackernoon.com/50-big-companies-that-started-with-little-or-no-money-4ef1b68aac25

Fletcher, David, 'Psychological Resilience and Adversarial Growth in Sport and Performance', *The Oxford Encyclopedia of Sport, Exercise, and Performance Psychology*, Oxford University Press (2019) https://www.researchgate.net/publication/333311716_Psychological_resilience_and_adversarial_growth_in_sport_and_performance

Flow Genome Project https://www.flowgenomeproject.com/

Gardner, Chris, 'Kristen Stewart Describes Karl Lagerfeld as "a compulsive and obsessive artist"', *Hollywood Reporter* (1 March 2017) https://www.hollywoodreporter.com/news/kristen-stewart-karl-lagerfeld-as-a-compulsive-obsessive-artist-982028

Gayford, Martin, 'How Veronese Outwitted the Inquisition', *Telegraph* (3 April 2014) http://www.telegraph.co.uk/culture/art/10663746/How-Veronese-outwitted-the-Inquisition.html

Gianoglio, Martina, 'Architecture, Design and Intelligent Systems: The Cybertecture Egg', *Living Map* (18 September 2017) https://www.livingmap.com/smart-building/the-cybertecture-egg-smart-building/

Goins, Jeff, 'The Story of the Starving Artist Needs to Die', *Better Marketing* (19 August 2019) https://medium.com/better-marketing/why-the-story-of-the-starving-artist-needs-to-die-6d69d7fbebea

Gompertz, Will, *What Are You Looking At?*, Penguin (2012)

Griffey, Harriet, 'The Lost Art of Concentration: Being Distracted in a Digital World', *Guardian* (14 October 2018) https://www.theguardian.com/lifeandstyle/2018/oct/14/the-lost-art-of-concentration-being-distracted-in-a-digital-world

Hagerty, James R., 'George Laurer, Defying Instructions, Created Universal Bar Code', *Wall Street Journal* (12 December 2019) https://www.wsj.com/articles/george-laurer-defying-instructions-created-universal-bar-code-11576183780

Hartmans, Avery, 'The Career Rise and Fabulous Life of Google Cofounder Larry Page', *Business Insider* (3 December 2019) http://uk.businessinsider.com/larry-page-alphabet-google-life-career-photos-2017-8

Hatfield, Rab, *The Wealth of Michelangelo*, Edizioni di Storia e Letteratura (2002)

Heathcote, Edwin, 'Architecture Explained – with the Help of Grayson Perry's Shrine', *Financial Times* (18 November 2015) https://www.ft.com/content/e5d781ce-8896-11e5-90de-f44762bf9896

Hegarty, John, '6 Ads That Made . . . Bartle Bogle Hegarty', *Campaign* (17 July 2014) http://www.campaignlive.co.uk/article/6-ads-made-bartle-bogle-hegarty/1303564

Hegde, Raghuraj, 'How Much Creativity Is Involved in Being a Doctor?', *Quora* (2016) https://www.quora.com/How-much-creativity-is-involved-in-being-a-doctor-That-is-how-often-do-you-have-to-come-up-with-creative-or-interesting-solutions-to-problems-when-youre-a-doctor-Or-is-everything-very-standardized

Herwig, Christopher, *Soviet Bus Stops*, Fuel (2015)

Hesse, Monica, 'Obama Honors Inventor of Digital Camera', *Washington Post* (22 November 2010) http://www.washingtonpost.com/wp-dyn/content/article/2010/11/22/AR2010112207556_2.html??noredirect=on

Hitti, Natashah, 'Amalia Shem Tov Designs "ancient" Cooking Utensils for the Modern Kitchen', *Dezeen* (22 August 2018) https://www.dezeen.com/2018/08/22/roots-ancient-cooking-utensils-shenkar-college-graduate-amalia-shem-tov/

Hitti, Natashah, 'IKEA and Tom Dixon Launch Modular Bed with Collection of "authorised hacks"', *Dezeen* (1 February 2018) https://www.dezeen.com/2018/02/01/ikea-tom-dixon-modular-delaktig-bed-authorised-hacks-furniture-design/

Holiday, Ryan, *Growth Hacker Marketing: A Primer on the Future of PR, Marketing and Advertising*, Profile Books (2014)

Holt, Elizabeth Gilmore, *A Documentary History of Art*, Princeton University Press (1947)

Howarth, Dan, 'Dezeen's A-Zdvent Calendar: Wiggle Chair by Frank Gehry', *Dezeen* (23 December 2014) https://www.dezeen.com/2014/12/23/a-zdvent-calendar-wiggle-chair-frank-gehry/

Jackson, Mark Allan, 'Prophet Singer: The Voice and Vision of Woody Guthrie', *LSU Digital Commons* (2002) https://digitalcommons.lsu.edu/cgi/viewcontent.cgi?article=1134&context=gradschool_dissertations

Jobs, Steve, 'Apple's One-Dollar-a-Year Man', *Fortune* (24 January 2000) https://archive.fortune.com/magazines/fortune/fortune_archive/2000/01/24/272277/index.htm

Jones, Jonathan, 'Heavenly Art', *Guardian* (6 March 2006) https://www.theguardian.com/culture/2006/mar/06/1

Jones, Quincy, 'Quincy Jones on Michael Jackson: "We made history together"', *Los Angeles Times* (29 June 2009) https://latimesblogs.latimes.com/music_blog/2009/06/quincy-jones-on-michael-jackson-we-owned-the-80s-and-our-souls-would-be-connected-forever.html

Journal of Consumer Research, 'Trying to Project an Image of Success? It Could Make You Dwell on Your Failures', *ScienceDaily* (22 January 2015) https://www.sciencedaily.com/releases/2015/01/150122084342.htm

Kachroo-Levine, Maya, 'The Incredible Reason Why Richard Branson Started Virgin Atlantic', *Travel + Leisure* (12 July 2019) https://www.travelandleisure.com/travel-tips/celebrity-travel/how-richard-branson-started-virgin-atlantic

Kaipa, Prasad and Radjou, Navi, '7 Business Decisions That Looked Bad but Turned Good', *CNBC* (14 April 2013) https://www.cnbc.com/id/100634625

Kellaway, Kate, 'Still Fresh as a Daisy: Mary Quant's Era-Defining Fashion', *Observer* (17 March 2019) https://www.theguardian.com/fashion/2019/mar/17/mary-quant-fresh-as-a-daisy-fashion-v-and-a-retrospective

Lindholm, Olle, '11 Important Life Lessons from Dr. Seuss', *Lifehack* https://www.lifehack.org/articles/communication/11-important-life-lessons-from-seuss.html

Ma, Moses, 'The Power of Humor in Ideation and Creativity', *Psychology Today* (17 June 2014) https://www.psychologytoday.com/us/blog/the-tao-innovation/201406/the-power-humor-in-ideation-and-creativity

Macaro, Antonia and Baggini, Julian, 'Is Balance Boring?', *Financial Times* (22 January 2016) https://www.ft.com/content/00a2a712-befd-11e5-9fdb-87b8d15baec2

Mander, Karel van, *Schilder-Boeck*, Passchier Wesbusch (1604)

Marr, David, *Vision: A Computational Investigation into the Human Representation and Processing of Visual Information*, W.H. Freeman and Company (1982)

McLaws Helms, Laura, 'The Mercurial, Obsessive Life of Karl Lagerfeld', *Heroine* (1 March 2019) https://www.heroine.com/the-editorial/karl-lagerfeld-career

Mendini, Alessandro, 'The Story of the Proust Chair', *Atelier Mendini* (15 June 2001) http://www.ateliermendini.it/index.php?mact=News,cntnt01,print,0&cntnt01articleid=147&cntnt01showtemplate=false&cntnt01returnid=67

Mitchell, Donald, 'Mahler and Freud', *Chord and Discord* 2(8) (1958)

MoMA, 'Gordon Matta-Clark: *Bingo*', *MoMA Highlights: 375 Works from The Museum of Modern Art*, MoMA Publications (2019) https://www.moma.org/collection/works/91762

Morin, Amy, '5 Ways Mentally Strong People Deal With Rejection', *Inc.* (11 November 2015) https://www.inc.com/amy-morin/5-ways-mentally-strong-people-deal-with-rejection.html

Murray, Ben, 'Remixing Culture and Why the Art of the Mash-Up Matters', *TechCrunch* (23 March 2015) https://techcrunch.com/2015/03/22/from-artistic-to-technological-mash-up/

Nastasi, Alison, '100 Famous Directors' Rules of Filmmaking', *Flavorwire* (11 July 2014) http://flavorwire.com/465913/100-famous-directors-rules-of-filmmaking/view-all

Norden, Eric, 'Playboy Interview: Stanley Kubrick', Playboy (September 1968) https://scrapsfromtheloft. com/2016/10/02/playboy-interview-stanley-kubrick/

Nowak, Peter, 'Digital Cameras: A Decade of Revolutionary Pictures', CBC (22 December 2009) https://www.cbc. ca/news/technology/digital-cameras-a-decade-of-revolutionary-pictures-1.793455

Overbeck, Jochen, 'Please, Have a Seat: Interview with Marianne Panton', Icon (March 2018) https://www.vitra. com/en-gb/magazine/details/please-have-a-seat

Pandey, Suresh K., Milverton, E. John, Maloof, Anthony J., 'A Tribute to Charles David Kelman MD', National Library of Medicine (October 2004) https://pubmed.ncbi.nlm.nih. gov/15498067/

Peacock, Louisa, 'Zaha Hadid Interview: "Women are always told they won't make it"', Telegraph (22 April 2013) https://www.telegraph.co.uk/women/womens-business/10011974/Zaha-Hadid-interview-Women-are-always-told-they-wont-make-it.html

Pelusi, Nando, 'Neanderthink: The Ups and Downs of Ambition', Psychology Today (1 May 2008) https://www. psychologytoday.com/gb/articles/200805/neanderthink-the-ups-and-downs-ambition

Penenberg, Adam, Viral Loop, Sceptre (2009)

Phelps, Nicole, 'Gucci Fall 2015 Ready-to-Wear', Vogue (25 February 2015) https://www.vogue.com/fashion-shows/fall-2015-ready-to-wear/gucci

Pollak, Michael, 'Dali on the Warpath', *New York Times* (5 November 2006) https://www.nytimes.com/2006/11/05/nyregion/thecity/05fyi.html

Pometsey, Olive, 'Studio now!', *Drugstore Culture* (2018)

Poynor, Rick, *Obey the Giant: Life in the Image World*, Birkhäuser (2007)

Quant, Mary, *Quant by Quant*, V&A Publishing (2018)

Ransley, Kim, and Holcombe, Alex O., 'What DO you see?', *Daily Mail* (25 July 2017) http://www.dailymail.co.uk/sciencetech/article-4728406/Illusions-reveal-hidden-workings-brain.html#ixzz552OFzXnn

Rettig, Tim, 'Living on the Margins: How to Be an Outsider and Still Be Happy', *Medium* (17 December 2017) https://medium.com/intercultural-mindset/living-on-the-margins-how-to-be-an-outsider-and-still-be-happy-f8d3e7b493c0

Rice-Oxley, Mark, '*Vorsprung durch Technik* – Ad Slogan That Changed How We Saw Germany', *Guardian* (18 September 2012) https://www.theguardian.com/world/2012/sep/18/vorsprung-durch-technik-advertising-germany

Rindskopf, Jeff, '6 Albums That Created Their Own New Genres', *Showbiz Cheatsheet* (30 December 2015) https://www.cheatsheet.com/entertainment/6-albums-that-created-their-own-new-genres.html/

Rivka, Sarah, 'Navigating Coppola's Maze: Editing in *The Godfather*', *The Godfather, Anatomy of a Film*, UC Berkeley (2018) http://theseventies.berkeley.edu/godfather/tag/baptism-scene/

Root-Bernstein, Robert, 'Arts Foster Scientific Success', *Journal of Psychology of Science and Technology*, Volume 1, Number 2 (2008) https://www.psychologytoday.com/files/attachments/1035/arts-foster-scientific-success.pdf

Rose, Todd, *The End of Average*, Penguin Books (2017)

Ross, Alex, *The Rest Is Noise*, HarperCollins (2007)

Russell, Kyle, '6 Amazing Ads Directors Made Before They Were Famous', *Business Insider* (21 July 2013) http://www.businessinsider.com/ads-by-directors-before-they-were-famous-2013-7?IR=T

Sala, Fabio, 'Laughing All the Way to the Bank', *Harvard Business Review* (September 2003) https://hbr.org/2003/09/laughing-all-the-way-to-the-bank

Sanderson, David, 'Eden Project Grew Out of a Lie, Admits Its Founder', *The Times* (10 October 2016) https://www.thetimes.co.uk/article/eden-project-grew-out-of-a-lie-admits-its-founder-n767sd93j

Sawyer, Keith, 'The Myth of Artistic Inspiration', *The Creativity Guru* (9 December 2012) https://keithsawyer.wordpress.com/2012/12/09/the-myth-of-artistic-inspiration/

Saymova, Valeriya, 'Ten Lessons of Successful Self-promotion from Salvador Dali', *Arthive* https://arthive.com/publications/2800~Ten_lessons_of_successful_selfpromotion_from_Salvador_Dali

Segun-Amao, Bimbola, 'The Richard Branson Wisdom: Never Say No to an Opportunity', *Pride Magazine Nigeria* (16 February 2015) http://www.pridemagazineng.com/opportunity/

Self, Will, 'David Shrigley: "I gave my book out at the pub – that's how it all started"', *Guardian* (18 October 2013) https://www.theguardian.com/artanddesign/2013/oct/18/david-shrigley-book-pub-started

Seuss, Dr (Theodor Seuss Geisel), various titles

Shafrazi, Tony, 'Keith Haring. A Great Artist, A True Friend', *The Keith Haring Foundation* (2005) https://www.haring.com/!/selected_writing/keith-haring-a-great-artist-a-true-friend#:~:text=His%20job%20at%20the%20gallery,his%20tools%20and%20brushes%20afterwards.

Shen, Yiling, 'Daniel Libeskind on the Poetics of Memory and Time in Architecture', *ArchDaily* (15 April 2018) https://www.archdaily.com/892325/daniel-libeskind-on-the-poetics-of-memory-and-time-in-architecture

Smith, Harrison, 'George Laurer, an Inventor of the Modern Bar Code, Dies at 94', *Washington Post* (10 December 2019) https://www.washingtonpost.com/local/obituaries/george-laurer-an-inventor-of-the-modern-bar-code-dies-at-94/2019/12/10/75b03f6e-1b5c-11ea-8d58-5ac3600967a1_story.html

Smith, Jacquelyn, '10 Reasons Why Humor Is a Key to Success At Work', *Forbes* (3 May 2013) https://www.forbes.com/sites/jacquelynsmith/2013/05/03/10-reasons-why-humor-is-a-key-to-success-at-work/#1ca5018b5c90

Solomons, Jason, 'Me and My Troll', *Observer* (4 July 2004) https://www.theguardian.com/film/2004/jul/04/features.review

Sooke, Alastair, 'From "son of India" to a Global Superstar', *Telegraph* (7 December 2010) https://www.telegraph.co.uk/culture/art/8186223/From-son-of-India-to-a-global-superstar.html

Starck, Philippe, *Harvard Business Review* (April 2013) https://hbr.org/2013/04/philippe-starck

Sudjic, Deyan, 'Obscure Objets of Desire', *Observer* (2 March 2003) https://www.theguardian.com/theobserver/2003/mar/02/2

Tate, 'The Story of Cold Dark Matter', *Tate*, https://www.tate.org.uk/art/artworks/parker-cold-dark-matter-an-exploded-view-t06949/story-cold-dark-matter

textbook.stpauls.br, 'Introduction to Business Management/Organisational Objectives AO2/Statements – Mission and Vision' http://textbook.stpauls.br/Business_Organization/page_37.htm

This is not ADVERTISING, 'Handbuilt by Robots – Collett Dickenson Pearce for Fiat Strada' (16 October 2014) https://thisisnotadvertising.wordpress.com/2014/10/16/handbuilt-by-robots-collett-dickenson-pearce-for-fiat-strada-1979/

Thomas, Michael, 'Why Kickstarter Decided to Radically Transform Its Business Model', *Fast Company* (12 April 2017) https://www.fastcompany.com/3068547/why-kickstarter-decided-to-radically-transform-its-business-model

Timmer, Sjors, 'Rem Koolhaas – Designing the Design Process', *Sjors Timmer blog* (7 February 2012) http://notura.com/2012/02/rem-koolhaas-designing-the-design-process/

Titner, Eric, 'How to Seamlessly Transfer Your Skills from One Industry to Another', *The Job Network* https://www.thejobnetwork.com/transfer-your-skills-from-one-industry-to-another/

University of Washington, 'Mapping American Social Movements Project' https://depts.washington.edu/moves/

Vigil, Joseph, 'Deconstructionism in Literature: Definition & Examples', *Study.Com* (2015) study.com/academy/lesson/deconstructionism-in-literature-definition-examples-quiz.html

Wainwright, Oliver, 'Soviet Superpower: Why Russia Has the World's Most Beautiful Bus Stops', *Guardian* (2 September 2015) https://www.theguardian.com/artanddesign/2015/sep/02/soviet-superpower-why-russia-has-the-worlds-most-beautiful-bus-stops

Wainwright, Oliver, 'Robert Venturi: The Bad-Taste Architect Who Took a Sledgehammer to Modernism', *Guardian* (20 September 2018) https://www.theguardian.com/artanddesign/2018/sep/20/robert-venturi-the-bad-taste-architect-who-took-a-sledgehammer-to-modernism

Walter, Aarron, 'Personality in Design', *A List Apart* (18 October 2011) https://alistapart.com/article/personality-in-design/

Warhol, Andy, *The Philosophy of Andy Warhol: From A to B and Back Again*, Penguin (2007)

Weir, Kirsten, 'More Than Job Satisfaction', *American Psychological Association* (December 2013) http://www.apa.org/monitor/2013/12/job-satisfaction.aspx

Whitworth, Damian, 'Beyond Caravaggio – the Old Master Uncovered', *The Times* (24 September 2016) https://www.thetimes.co.uk/article/the-excess-and-vulgarity-is-what-the-modern-world-likes-about-caravaggio-m3n0x5stn

Wilson, Matt, 'A Joke Turned into a Multi-Million Dollar Business', *Under30CEO* (4 March 2014) https://under30ceo.com/joke-turned-multi-million-dollar-business-interview-omar-tayeb-blippar/

In the chapter on Dr Seuss, the drawing of the head of a character is my interpretation of the style of Dr Seuss.

The drawing in Chihuly chapter is my illustration of an anemone, the kind of sea creature that inspired Chihuly.